Facebook Marketing and Advertising for Small Business Owners

Discover How to Optimize the

Money You Spend on Facebook And

Get Maximum Results By Using

Proven ROI Methods

Mark Warner

book.

By reading this document, the reader agrees that under no circumstances is the author responsible for any losses, direct or indirect, which are incurred as a result of the use of the information contained within this document, including, but not limited to, — errors, omissions, or inaccuracies.

Table of Contents

Introduction   **13**

Principles to Power Your Facebook Strategy   13

Checklist for Creating & Optimizing Facebook Ads   19

Choosing an Editor   20

Choose Your Ad Objective   21

Choose Your Audience   22

Setting Your Budget   23

Schedule   24

Pricing   24

Creating Your Ad   24

Ad Performance   26

Facebook Ad Manager   26

Marketing Software Ads   27

Marketing Plan   27

Goals   28

Your Target Audience   29

Set a Budget   29

Create and Planning Engaging Content   30

Monitor Your Progress   31

Split Testing   31

Social Media Script   32

Facebook Facts   36

How Facebook Helps Small Businesses   38

What Users Are Looking for on Facebook   39

Success Stories   41

Toyota Israel   43

Chapter 1: How to Influence People?   **45**

Start a Conversation   45

Motivate People   46

Make Customers Support Your Story   46

Provide Quality Content   46

Make Customer Service Your Regular Routine   47

Experiment with Videos   47

Use the Insight   48

Target the Right Audience   48

Principles of Persuasion   49

Chapter 2 - The Foundation   **55**

The Important Buyer Persona Questions That You Need To Ask 55

A Basic Buy Persona Template Example   61

Pain Points and Goals   62

Real Estate Example   63

Pain Points and Goals   65

Restaurant Example   65

Pain Points and Goals   67

Chapter 3: Start Growing Your Business with Facebook   **69**

What Content Can You Create On Facebook   69

How to Effectively Market With Facebook   70

Facebook Marketing Advantages   70

Paid Content Vs Organic Content   72

Creating A Facebook Business Account   73

Creating Your Account   74

Assigning Levels   74

Add a Payment Method   75

Creating a Facebook Company Fan Page   75

Enter Basic Information   76

Use the Admin Panel   77

Tell Stories   77

Build Tabs to Generate Sales   78

Facebook Marketing Tips for Small Businesses   78

Post with Intent   79

Try To Blend In   79

Don't Forget Your Content Calendar   79

Optimize Your Profile Page   80

Clear the Community Page   80

Create a Facebook Group   80

Strategically Choose Your Name   81

Use the Facebook story to your advantage   81

Start With One Advertisement At A Time On A Limited Budget   82

Consider Boosting Posts   82

Biggest mistakes you make on Your Facebook Profile & Fan Page   83

Posting too many times on Facebook   83

Not Engaging In Comments   83

Arguing   84

Deleting negative comments   84

Running competitions against the rules   84

Posting similar content   85

Not using applications properly   85

Not responding   86

Generating traffic to your website   86

The Most Common Persuasion Mistakes   87

Validating undesirable   87

Highlight gain instead of the loss   88

Misusing your authority   89

The principle of liking   89

Enforcing the principle of consistency   90

Not giving a reason   90

Proven Ways to Boost Organic (Non-Paid) Facebook Posts   91

Analyze Your Top 10   91

Post amazing content   91

Optimize targeting   92

Don't cross-post   92

Learn the best times to post   92

Share on weekends as well   93

Make the most of Facebook live   93

Use your blog posts to your advantage   93

Use events to your advantage   94

Make use of webinars   94

Email marketing   95

Using Pinterest   95

Ask your fans to enable notifications   95

Facebook Engagement Tactics for Your Business Page   96

Collect questions in comments   96

Share offers about products to anyone who pings you on messenger   97

Use emojis to your advantage   97

Shout out to customers   97

Run a contest!   98

Ask for feedback   98

Share relevant information   99

Ask open-ended questions   99

Start Joining Conversations That Are Relevant   100

Speak About Your Community Involvement   100

Don't be serious all the time   101

Examples of Interactive Facebook Posts   101

Scroll Stopping Content   103

Why do people share content?   103

Targeting on Facebook   105

Chapter 4: How to Set up Facebook Business Manager   **107**

Create Your Facebook Business Manager Account   107

Add Your Business Page   108

Add Your Facebook Ad Account   108

Add People to Help Manage the Facebook Business Page   109

Assign People to Manage Your Facebook Page   109

Link to Your Instagram Account   110

Setting Up Facebook Pixels   111

Placing Your Ad   112

Reasons You Should Be Advertising on Facebook   112

Benefits of the Facebook Pixel   115

Chapter 5: Choose The Best Advertising Option For Your Business on Facebook   **119**

Video Ad   119

Photo Ad   120

Reach Ad   120

Offer Ad   121

Event Ad   121

Retargeting Ad   122

Targeting Based On The Audience   122

Chapter 6: Ideas And Tips For Ads Using The Persuasion Principles   **125**

Reciprocity   125

Consistency and Commitment   126

Social Proof   127

The Principle of Liking   128

Authority   128

Scarcity   129

Chapter 7: When It All Comes Together: The Plan   **131**

Implement an organized Content Strategy   131

Save On Time   132

Create Content Well In Advance   133

You Can Create A Strategy   133

Stop Building Facebook Apps   134

Picking the Wrong Prize For Your Contest   134

Post Educational Content   135

Stop Wasting Time on Facebook   135

Don't Purchase Fans   136

Get More Out Of Your Ad Results   136

Chapter 8: Email and Email marketing   **139**

Facebook Marketing Versus Email Marketing   139

Getting Traffic to Your Facebook Ads   141

Create a Landing Page within Your Facebook Ad   142

Create the Right Campaign For Your Email Ids   143

Ways to Collect Leads From Your Facebook Campaign   143

Chapter 9: Improve, Test, Grow, and Monetize   **147**

Mix Up Your Content   147

Encourage Posts from Your Fans   148

Use Contest in Moderation   148

Create Interesting Content   149

Define your USP   149

Targeting Current Customers   151

The Ladder of Engagement   153

Tell Stories as Part of Your Facebook Campaign   155

How To Stop People From Scrolling Past Your Post?   157

Create Engaging Video Content   159

Understanding Content Marketing   161

Look For Inspiration   163

Conclusion   **167**

Bibliography   **171**

Introduction

Principles to Power Your Facebook Strategy

Marketing your business on Facebook can be very effective. If you are a small organization looking to expand your horizons, there is no better place for you to begin with than Facebook. It's a strong platform and with a little effort and the right persuasion skills, not only will you be able to market your business but also establish a brand that becomes popular in a short time span.

It is important to have an online presence if you want to stay in competition today and the best way for you to do this is to start marketing your business on social media platforms where most of the population spends its time. Facebook has over 1.7 billion people and that comprises almost 25% of the entire population of the earth. When it comes to marketing your business, not only is Facebook a great platform but it's also time-saving and helps you invest your money where you can get returns, thereby making it a profitable solution. However, if you want to make sure your marketing efforts do not go in vain you need the right Facebook strategy and principles to help you come up with a plan that accomplishes your goals and visions. Here are some interesting principles that you should base your Facebook marketing strategy that will help you create posts and content that's persuasive and helps increase your customer base.

Try Out Your Business First

Whether you are a service-based business or you are trying to sell products, always make sure you have complete knowledge of your business. It's important for you to first try your business out before you go out to the public and tell them to get involved with it. Once you know your business, it helps you to answer any questions that are thrown at you.

Apart from being able to identify the benefits and the USP of your business, you will also get to know any potential issues that may need to be rectified before it hits the audience. Marketing on a social media platform is great, but it comes at a price and if your business is not up to the mark, people are going to be vocal about it on the same platform. To put it in simple words, make sure you have all your corners covered and you start promoting your business on Facebook confidently, knowing that you are selling a strong brand to the audience.

Update Yourself with Information

Understand how social media interaction works so that you figure out a plan for your business and make the most out of each interaction in order for your marketing efforts to pay off.

Learn more about Facebook analytics and the wide variety of different tools that Facebook offers to get data-driven results and figure out what strategies work best for your business.

Create A Personality for Your Brand

Instead of trying to blend in with the crowd, you need to focus on standing out and Facebook will be able to do this for you when you establish a brand that's different from the others. Do something unique and have your own identity that helps you differ from other businesses that are similar in nature to your business. If you do the same thing they are doing, you are not going to get different results. Your results are based on the effort you put into your marketing and the strategies you apply. You have to be a little persuasive, a little unique, and bold if you want to make a mark on Facebook.

Interaction Is Important

Most business owners think that Facebook is a one-way communication platform and post what they want to say to potential customers and wait for results to kick in. If you want people to show an interest in your business you have to interact with them and be available to answer queries or to give them solutions for problems they may be facing. Interacting with the audience makes it easy to increase your potential customers. You can always initiate an interaction by asking questions or creating a poll on your Facebook page to gather attention.

Creating A Community

Facebook allows you to express yourself and create a sense of community amongst your target audience. With Facebook, you are not limited to the number of characters you post, neither are you limited to sharing only certain images or certain posts. You can tell a story to your audience with the help of your Facebook posts and give them an idea of what your business is all about. This will help them connect with your business and become a brand. Share personal stories and involve the audience in your success. The way this can be done is by listening to your fans and respecting their opinions. You can start sharing success stories about people that your brand has helped. For example, if you are a shoe company, you can share stories where you have helped certain people with your products. There are various people out there that cannot afford expensive branded shoes. You can sponsor such a community with your shoes and share your story with the rest of the world. This will create a feel-good factor amongst your audience and it will also motivate them to do something good for others in society. Don't complicate your ideas too much. Just communicate from your heart and your audience will relate to you.

Be Kind to Your Audience

Facebook marketing is all about communicating with your audience for their benefit. You do not have to spam someone's news feed in order to get your brand name out there. You need to start sharing and interacting with people with a view to benefiting. When you start providing value, your audience will start paying attention. You should look to write for your potential customers rather than writing for yourself. Try to find out what your audience would love to hear and how you can benefit them through your brand. Show your audience that you are committed to their wellbeing and you will be able to connect with them emotionally.

If you are a local brand you should display fan stories on your Facebook page. These stories can highlight the heroes in your locality and show everyone the kindness that they have displayed. These could be local inspirations or heroic deeds that have helped the community. Help these heroes become an influencer within your community circle and start making a difference to the community. If you are a big national brand then you need to reach out to the people that communicate with you and thank them personally. How many times have you written to a brand and they have not bothered replying to you, apart from the standard auto-reply that you received? Start personalizing messages and see how much human interaction can help your brand go viral.

Be Transparent

Facebook marketing is all about transparency. A classic example is receiving a negative comment on any of your posts or your business page. The first reaction would be to lash out at this post or to delete it so that others will not be able to see it. However, the sensible thing to do would be to treat the comment with respect and respond immediately. If your business made a mistake you need to own up to it and apologize to your customers. You should also try to post about the mistake on your own rather than waiting for bad publicity to take its own course.

Make People Laugh

Yes, the world of marketing and branding is a very serious business but focusing on humor is extremely essential. You need to find the right balance between being serious and making people laugh every once in a while. If you only post about things that make people laugh, no one will take your brand seriously. But if you keep posting serious things on your Facebook page, your fans may shy away. One classic example is the ALS ice bucket challenge. This brand took a very serious issue such as a brain disease and communicated the seriousness with a fun challenge. Soon there were millions of people pouring ice water on their head and these are the kind of posts that you need to target.

Be Clear About What You Expect

While your Facebook page may get a lot of attention and you will get a lot of followers, you need to tell your customers what you are expecting from them. This means you need certain 'call to action' buttons around your fan page that will ask your fans to either visit your website or to read your blog post or to share your post or even purchase your product. You need to let your fans know that they have the power to make a difference and you need to empower them by giving them the ability to make your post go viral. As complicated as it sounds, it is a very smart way of convincing your reader that he or she can contribute towards an internet sensation.

Checklist for Creating & Optimizing Facebook Ads

A Guide On Performing The Basic Facebook Actions

It is important to create a Facebook ad in the right manner and there are a number of steps involved. You need to see if you are targeting the right audience, if your image meets the dimensions, or if you are selecting the right kind of ad. If you are doing all of this for the first time, it can get extremely confusing. There are over a billion people using Facebook and almost all of them visit it on a daily basis. This is what makes Facebook the perfect platform to market your business and become an overnight sensation. The flip side to this is that if something goes wrong or you are not creating the right kind of ads, there is very little that you can do to rectify it because of the number of people that would have seen the ad. You need to be accurate with regards to your ad creation and make sure that you keep the steps in mind before you publish your ad.

Your Facebook ad can be broken down into three categories:

- **Campaign:** This will define your assets.
- **Ad sets:** If you want to target separate audiences across different geographies and other sectors, then you will want separate ad sets for each.
- **The actual ads:** Your ads are the actual images or posts that go out to the customers within each ad set.

Now let us look at how to create effective Facebook ads with tools that are provided by Facebook.

Choosing an Editor

There are two editors that are available to all Facebook users that will help create a paid ad. The first is the ads manager and the other is the power editor. You need to select an editor based on the number of words that you want to run as well as the size of your company. The ads manager is ideal for most of the companies out there while the power editor is ideal for large businesses that want control over their ad campaigns.

Since this book deals with helping small businesses create a brand via Facebook, we will focus on the ads manager editor.

Choose Your Ad Objective

When you start with Facebook ads manager it will ask you for your objective for the campaign. There are 10 different objectives you could choose from. These include

- Sending people to your website
- Boost your posts
- Increase your website conversion
- Promoting your page
- Get users to download and install your app
- Increase app engagement
- Connect with people located close to your business
- Increased attendance for an event that you are organizing
- Get more people to claim any offers that you are offering
- To get video views

When you pick one of these objectives, Facebook will get a better idea of what you are trying to do and the best ad-options depending on your objective. Let us take an example. Assume you selected 'driving more traffic to your website' as your objective. Once you've selected this objective, Facebook will ask you to enter the URL you want to promote. Once you have entered the URL, Facebook will provide a list of the ad-options that will help achieve this objective.

Choose Your Audience

If you using Facebook Ads for the first time it will be difficult for you to select a target audience because you are not sure of how it will work. It's best to select different targeting options until you get the right mix and you find the audience that suits your requirements. Facebook also helps you narrow down your focus by providing you with filter options to help define your audience. When you select the criteria for your audience and you enter all the fields, you will be able to see your potential reach number.

You can play with the options available until you reach the ideal number and use 'select the right audience', keeping your objective in mind. If you just want people to get to your website you may want to target specific people that are interested in what you are offering. If you are looking to build brand awareness then you may want to target a general audience so that the outreach is not limited. Facebook has a number of built-in targeting options you can choose from. Some of the options include:

- Age
- Location
- Language
- Gender

- Education
- Relationship
- Finances
- Work
- Ethnicity
- Home
- Parents
- Life events
- Behavior
- Interests
- Connections

You can take a custom audience based on the kind of people you are targeting. You can build this custom audience with the help of your company database and get specific people to your business page. Once this is created on your Facebook page you may want to keep trying it with different groups until you find a group that is responding to your ads. You can create multiple groups and see which of them have responded to your ads better.

Setting Your Budget

Facebook allows you to select two kinds of budgets - setting a daily budget or setting a lifetime budget. The daily budget will make your ad run continuously during the day. When you select a daily budget Facebook will paste your ads on a daily basis, keeping your budget in mind. It allows Facebook to post your ads across a period of time rather than posting it daily. Once you pay for a specific period, Facebook will make sure that the ad runs uniformly across this period, keeping in mind peak hours as well as the audience.

Schedule

Once you select your budget and your campaign you then need to select whether you want the campaign to run right now or you want to customize the dates. You can select the parameters with regards to the times you want the campaign to run or specific days of the week.

Pricing

You can either choose to pay for your objective, your clicks, or your impressions. Based on the pricing model that you select, Facebook will decide when to display ads and to whom. Facebook will even provide you with a suggestion for the pricing based on behavior towards other advertisers.

Creating Your Ad

Your ad needs to match your objective. If you want to increase the number of clicks for your blog or your website then you will need to select a 'click to website' ad-option. There are two ad-options that you get. You can either pick a link or a carousel. Link a single image ad that will direct customers to your website. A carousel will be a multi-image ad that will also have a link to direct people to your website. There are design criteria that you need to adhere to for each of the two formats. For a single image ad you need to keep the following criteria in mind:

- text no more than 90 characters.
- link title no more than 25 characters.
- image ratio needs to be 1.91:1.
- the image size needs to be 1200 pixels by 627 pixels.

For a carousel ad you need to keep the following criteria in mind:

- The image size needs to be 600 pixels by 600 pixels.
- the image ratio needs to be 1:1.
- text shall not exceed 90 characters.
- the headline should not be more than 40 characters.
- link description should not be more than 20 characters.
- the image cannot have more than 20% text.

These are only the options when you select the objective as 'send people to your website'. If you select a different objective you will get different ad-options. Each of these options has a different set of requirements and you need to explore all of them before picking the right advertising option. Once you select the type of ad, Facebook ads manager will help you with regards to the display of your ad. You can either from a desktop news feed, a mobile news feed, or a desktop right column.

If you have not created a Facebook page to associate with your ad you will only be able to create a desktop right ad column. If you want all three ad-options then you need to create a Facebook page for your business.

Ad Performance

Once your ad is live you will need to keep checking how it is performing and what the results look like. You will get the results in two places – one is your Facebook ad manager and the other would be your marketing software.

Facebook Ad Manager

The Facebook ad manager comes with a dashboard that will help you get an overview of all the campaigns running. The dashboard will show you how much you spend each day and you can filter your ads and customize the results too. You will get to see the reach, the frequency and the cost for each of the ads. You need to look at the performance of your ad and the engagement. If you have put up a video then you can see the percentage of people who viewed the full video and percentage of people who scrolled past. You can see the clicks to your website as well as the number of downloads for your mobile app. If you have created an event then you will be able to see the response for the event and the cost per response.

Marketing Software Ads

If you are not sure how to use Facebook ad manager then you can also use your marketing software to see the performance of your ads. Your marketing software will help you analyze the performance of an ad with the help of your URL. This will give you an idea of how many leads you have generated and how many of these leads are converted into customers. After reading this book, you will be able to put the following plans into action:

- Creating A Marketing Plan
- Picking The Right Social Media Script

Marketing Plan

There are over 2 billion monthly users on Facebook, making it the most popular social media platform you can use to market your business. However, the competition in this platform is fierce and if you want to make your business stand out amongst multiple other businesses marketing their products or services on Facebook you need a strategic marketing plan that works in your favor.

There are a number of small businesses on Facebook that looks to grow by using Facebook marketing to their advantage. If you are convinced Facebook marketing is the way you want to go then here are some effective marketing strategies to help your business become a visible brand online.

Goals

Before you pick any marketing strategy on Facebook, you need to set a realistic goal to achieve. Ask yourself why you want to market your business on Facebook and what you want to achieve by it. Some businesses look to create brand awareness, while others look to obtain leads that they can later convert into customers, while some people simply look to increase website traffic. Every business owner has a different goal and your marketing strategy should be based according to your goal.

You need to remember that there are no Facebook strategies that work well for all businesses and your goals need to be set in order for you to gain the most out of the activity that is specifically designed to benefit your business through Facebook marketing. When you plan to pick a goal you should always use the SMART goal strategy. This is easy to achieve and an effective way to transform your goal into reality. It focuses on the following

- Specific
- Measurable
- Achievable
- Realistic
- Timely

The reason the strategy is effective is that it helps you understand exactly what you want and it ensures that you take one step at a time to get where you want to be. It's specific because you can measure it and you know exactly how well you are doing with the plan in place. It also gives you a clear insight with regards to whether or not a strategy is actually working.

Your Target Audience

Yes, Facebook has over 2 billion users on a monthly basis, but all these people are not your target audience. When you are a small local business you need to focus on people who actually matter to your business and who can help you generate revenue. Whether it's geographical-bound or gender-bound it is always important you narrow down your target audience, applying as many filters as possible. Facebook ads manager gives you the option of figuring out what kind of audience you would like to choose and this helps you to market your business to the right people without spending unnecessary money on irrelevant customers that won't help your business grow.

Set a Budget

It is important for every business small or large to have a specific budget set aside for Facebook marketing so you don't go overboard with your marketing expenses and you manage to track whether or not the attempt was a profitable one or not. While it's good to invest money on Facebook marketing, it is important for you not to put all your eggs in one basket without knowing whether or not it's going to benefit you.

Create and Planning Engaging Content

It's not just about posting on Facebook but about what you post, which is why the content needs to be well planned, taking into consideration your goal, the budget, and the audience you plan on targeting.

It is important to keep pointers to help you create content that is highly engaging to the audience.

- Images with people's faces on them gain more attention
- A brighter and clearer image works well
- Stock photos never work for Facebook marketing
- Create videos that can be viewed with the sound off just as effectively as with the sound on. Only 15% of Facebook videos are watched with the sound turned on.
- People tend to get bored really fast so don't create a video that's so long, people end up losing interest in watching it completely. Post something that's fast, interactive, and intuitive.
- Post engagement advertisements

While it's important to create engaging content on your Facebook page you need to focus on the quality of the advertisements as well. Keep in mind the above information and use it for your Facebook advertisements to get better results. Remember, there are certain rules you have to follow when it comes to pictures on Facebook and so goes through them in detail before posting an image that might get rejected.

Monitor Your Progress

The only way you will be able to figure out whether or not your Facebook marketing strategies are paying off is when you monitor your progress on a regular basis. Doing it daily is highly recommended because you can change or spruce up your post depending on what you think may work better for the business, and this experimentation eventually leads to a foolproof Facebook marketing strategy that helps your business grow.

Split Testing

Always create two Facebook posts and label them as post-A and post-B. Measure the results for both posts to see how they perform and eliminate the one with the lower result. Continue repeating the split test using the higher result test against a new test until you figure out which Facebook strategy fits your business plan perfectly.

It's easy to measure progress because the Facebook ads manager provides you with complete statistics and reports that you can use to compare.

Social Media Script

Facebook is a large platform to market your business and, with the help of the right tools, not only will you be able to achieve your goals but you will also get closer to achieving business success. Most business owners use Facebook ads manager to effectively schedule and plan marketing strategies on Facebook. If you want to do something unique then a Facebook script add-on tool is something that not only helps you plan out of the box but makes it a little easier for you to deal with the various marketing campaigns you can share on Facebook regularly. Here are a few Facebook scripts you could give a try.

AdEspresso

Facebook ads manager could get a little difficult for some people and if you find it too complicated, AdEspresso is an amazing replacement that can help you to manage your campaigns on Facebook. The script allows you to optimize, analyze, and even execute your campaigns effectively. It also has the A/B testing capability that allows you to compare the various advertisements you post on Facebook to pick out the best ones.

AgoraPulse

This is a simple effective tool you can use that helps you to manage content and engage more people on Facebook. Right from scheduling your posts, to publishing them at a particular time, and monitoring the engagement for various posts AgoraPulse is a simple tool that can be used for your Facebook marketing plans. The highlight of this tool is that it has to keep tabs on your competition and get a fair idea of what strategies they are using on Facebook.

Buffer

Buffer is an interesting script you can integrate into your browser. It's really simple to use and it gives you complete analytics and insights on every post, helping you understand your marketing strategies in detail.

Driftrock

If lead generation is your main aim via Facebook marketing then the Driftrock FB script is something you should definitely give a try. Not only does it help you to create ads fast but it gives you various options to try out so that you can optimize your advertisement campaign and get better results.

DrumUp

Hashtags and emojis have gained a lot of popularity, and if you want to incorporate emojis in your Facebook post then

DrumUp is something that you must try. These different kinds, mostly emojis, are interesting and this unique feature helps to make your post stand out amongst the rest.

Fanpage Karma

If you want your business to grow, you need to understand your customers a little better. Fanpage Karma gives you insightful information about your fans and followers, helping you to understand them better and to service them more effectively. It also helps you to see what your competitors are doing and whether their advertisements are more successful than yours.

Heyo

Heyo is another interesting social media tool you can use if you are looking to generate leads. This marketing tool helps you to create various campaigns for your Facebook page and it also drives more engagement focusing on the right kind of users. Heyo is one of the few social media scripts that can help to create brand awareness as well as product awareness in the market.

Hootsuite

If you're looking for an analytical tool that can help you with Facebook marketing and optimize your campaign from time to time then Hootsuite is one of the most interesting Facebook scripts that you can use. Not only does it focus on lead generation but it also helps in better interaction and engagement because of the scheduling option it offers.

Likealyzer

It is important for you to get insights about your Facebook page so that you know how effective your marketing efforts are and what needs to be changed. Likealyzer not only helps you to get these insights but it gives you updates on your page, which determines whether your page is a good Facebook page or it needs improvement.

Meet Edgar

If you are looking for hassle-free and convenient management and scheduling tool then Meet Edgar is definitely something you should try. It helps you save a lot of time because it has an auto-fill feature that automatically fills using already entered information in the past.

Pagemodo

It's important for your Facebook page to stand out, and to be able to do this customization is vital. Pagemodo helps you customize your Facebook page with different impressive photo covers, tabs, as well as helps to organize contests to enhance the engagement.

Post Planner

Post Planner helps you to understand your publishing calendar and post-good-quality content until you reach maximum engagement for each post.

Facebook Facts

Facebook was only supposed to be a passing phase and a number of people didn't even register on Facebook when it first began. While this was something that only college students wanted to try out, it eventually expanded into something massive and today people cannot imagine their lives without Facebook. Apart from being a social media giant, Facebook also helps the number of communities across the world. Many small businesses have also turned to Facebook to build a brand name and go viral overnight.

Here is a look at the facts that make up Facebook and the mind-numbing numbers that many of you may not be aware of.

Facebook has over 1.3 billion users and these users are spread across the world. There are various family members and friends that live across borders and still manage to stay connected with the help of Facebook.

- it is said that almost 20000 people Login to Facebook every second. This means that 11 million users stay connected on FB every 18 minutes.

- every minute there are almost half a million users accessing Facebook on their smartphone.
- almost 80% of Facebook users access it from their phones.
- Facebook has the most mobile users across the globe and this number adds up to 740 million.
- Facebook messenger is one of the most used messengers and there are over 150,000 messages exchanged every minute.
- 49 million posts go up every 15 minutes. This boils down to 3 million posts every minute.
- there are close to 100,000 friend requests sent every 10 minutes.
- Facebook posts receive almost half a million likes every minute.
- in terms of generating revenue, Facebook helps to generate almost 1.4 million dollars every hour.
- most of the advertising revenue on Facebook comes from mobile ads.
- Facebook manages to earn 2.5 billion dollars through mobile advertising every quarter.
- over 350 million photos are uploaded on a daily basis on Facebook.
- almost 31% of the senior citizen population in the United States is on Facebook.
- the millennial (15 to 34 years) population accounts for

66% of Facebook users.

- The Asia Pacific has the largest number of Facebook users and they total up to over 450 million.
- Europe has the second largest number of users and this number is close to 300 million.
- USA and Canada have about 200 million users on Facebook while the rest of the world has about 400 million users.

How Facebook Helps Small Businesses

Small businesses have started realizing the potential with Facebook marketing and they have now started using it to their advantage. Almost 75% of all small businesses use social media to promote their brand as well as increase sales. Social media has become a necessity today and a number of small businesses are using these strategies to get a brand name and connect with their audience. When it comes to various social media channels, Facebook is number one followed by Instagram, YouTube, Twitter, LinkedIn, and Snapchat.

When it comes to gender, it is seen that women are more likely to use Facebook compared to men. This can be attributed to the fact that women are better at socializing and conversing with their customers than men. Women love expressing their emotions and female business owners are making the most of Facebook to promote their business. When it comes to age groups, millennial businesses use Facebook more than any other age group out there. Almost half the businesses post on Facebook on a daily basis. Amongst these users, half of them use images and infographics while the others post about offers on promotions that are coming up.

What Users Are Looking for on Facebook

Once you understand what people look for on social media you will be able to provide them with posts that help in better engagement and benefit your business in the long run. If you were to figure out what people are looking for, you'll be able to provide it to them and create posts that make them engage with your business. Here are a few things that you should always try to incorporate in your posts for better engagement.

Information

Social media is a great way to share information about products, offers, and services and a great place to give people what they are looking for. You need to provide your users with as much information as possible in the least amount of words so that you don't take up too much of their time but give them what's important for them to know.

Inspiration

Everyone is looking for a little inspiration every day and when you can do that in the form of a motivational video or a beautiful quote with a certain call to action it will benefit your business greatly. When you tug on to the emotional strings of the heart of a person, the chances of that post being shared automatically increase.

Offers

This is a great way to market your business on Facebook because you don't really have to invest too much money to grab attention. Exciting offers and discounts are something everyone looks forward to, and not only does this help to engage more people, but it also establishes a strong relationship between the customer and the business. When you provide special offers from time to time it increases customer loyalty and you have a stronger chance of repeat business.

Educational

People love learning new things, and sharing informative or educational posts from time to time can work really well. A small DIY project using certain products from your business or tips and tricks on how the services of your business will come in handy are some exciting ways to share information that will grab the attention of people on Facebook.

Humor

Tickling the funny bone has never failed to impress people, and whether you share a funny video, a joke, or even a name it's sure to be popular on Facebook.

How To

How-To's are really interesting, especially when it comes to teaching people about a product because it gives them more information. Visualization of a product helps to increase the sales and how-to videos can definitely get you the kind of popularity you are seeking from a post.

When you share information on Facebook you need to make sure it's not monotonous because that makes people bored and they tend to lose interest. Always try to come up with interesting and innovative ideas that can engage more people and increase your fan following on Facebook.

Success Stories

Styleshare

Styleshare Is a Korean fashion brand that successfully used the Facebook marketing strategy to not only help them to get 15 times the amount they invested as returns but a 60% click-through rate to encourage people to install their applications. They also had an increase in 25% of people who downloaded their applications in comparison to the previous year.

The business was established in 2011 and became an e-commerce business in 2016. As soon as Styleshare became an online brand they started marketing on Facebook. Their main goal was to increase the number of shoppers online to reduce physical storage and added expenses.

They targeted people between the age group of 18 and 37 and divided them into 4 groups

- Potential customers
- People using the application but not yet purchased from it
- People who added products to their cart but haven't completed the transaction
- Existing customers for their business

They planned their marketing strategy based on a carousel format that encouraged people to download the application. After they had a certain amount of people who successfully downloaded the application they then introduced app re-installation encouragement by telling people about special offers and discounts.

They came up with some creative advertisements from time to time to constantly engage the public, and not only did these advertisements include images but also contained videos.

They used the carousel method and displayed multiple images in one advertisement.

They displayed the collection of their products to lure people to download their app.

They used the dynamic app feature to personalize advertisement without too much effort.

They customized their audience preferences by filtering the ones that fit into their bracket the best.

They used a Facebook pixel to measure how effective the response was.

They even tested multiple social media platforms and marketing strategies but finally came to the realization that Facebook is a great place to persuade customers into purchasing and downloading the application, making the process a successful one.

Toyota Israel

Toyota Israel had one of the most successful Facebook ad campaigns when they planned to introduce advanced features on their popular car model. The campaign managed to boost their purchases by a staggering 48% and increased 33% in Agri fall, making it one of the most successful campaigns on Facebook. They also had an 80% brand lift in the automotive industry.

Toyota Israel focused on one particular car model - the Corolla and focused on the unique features and style of the car as its USP. People needed to know just what the car has in store, which is why they tried to incorporate as many video advertisements as possible. All of these videos were high-definition, bright, and spectacular in content, making them attractive in nature.

Unlike Styleshare, Toyota Israel chose to go a different route and they only introduced multiple video advertisements and focused on a wider audience to view the advertisements. In the end, they used the Facebook pixel to measure their activities and see how effective it was.

Chapter 1: How to Influence People?

Facebook helps a number of businesses grow and become successful with the right marketing strategies in place. It's important for you to persuade people to follow and like your Facebook business page, but it all begins with the right influence. If you want people to engage in your desired goal for your marketing plan you have got to influence them in that manner. Here are some interesting ways to influence people and benefit your business.

Start a Conversation

You need to let customers know how important they are to you and the best way to do it is to interact and converse. Communication is important and this doesn't just mean asking them to comment on your posts but rather interact with you and converse with them rather than having a one-sided communication with the posts you share. You should try to have a debate or a poll on your page from time to time or even ask questions and look forward to hearing from your customers or potential customers have to say because this will give you more insights on what they like and helps you to influence them better.

Motivate People

Motivation is really important if you want your business to grow, and in order for you to get the maximum benefit out of any marketing campaign, you have got to motivate people in a persuasive and subtle manner to carry out the call to action.

Make Customers Support Your Story

You have to tell people how happy your existing customers are with your business. Try asking customers to give you a testimonial or write a review for your business and share that on your social media page along with a tag to the customer. Not only does this increased reliability but it makes the brand more relatable and increases the value of your brand at the end of the day. Reviews and testimonials play a huge role in positively impacting your business so you need to make sure you use it in the right way to get the results you are seeking.

Provide Quality Content

Whatever your business is into, make sure you share quality content that is useful to the audience. When businesses know that you are the place to go to for quality content, you will automatically have more followers on your business page and people will start relying on your solutions. This makes it easy for you to promote your own brand without sounding too pushy.

Make Customer Service Your Regular Routine

If you want your business to double you need to service your customers effectively, and this doesn't stay limited to your website but it should be extended to your Facebook page as well. Not only should you be ready to reply to any queries but you should also resolve comments or issues that potential customers or existing customers have with a business. Whenever you are dealing with customers or potential customers, make sure to have a positive approach, no matter how negative the situation is.

Experiment with Videos

Videos are fairly new on Facebook and a lot of business owners are not very comfortable with the idea of investing money to show videos on their page. Statistically, videos are more likely to get engagement in comparison to posts, so the best way to start influencing the audience is to share videos that are of good quality.

Use the Insight

If you continue marketing your business without knowing whether or not your efforts are fruitful you will end up wasting a lot of money on something that might not necessarily be beneficial for you. You need to figure out whether or not you are influencing people in the right way and whether you need to change your marketing strategies to get more likes.

Target the Right Audience

This may sound too harsh but sometimes a small mistake with the filters you choose could end up getting you an irrelevant target audience that won't benefit your business in any way. Most small businesses are geographically-bound. Promoting your business on Facebook without selecting the right filters means you may end up getting audiences from different parts of the world. While this will help create awareness about your business, it will not help in terms of any revenue generation.

When you come up with a Facebook marketing strategy it doesn't only have to be one that works but it also needs to be one that manages to benefit your business, influencing it in the right way. Once you find the perfect balance between persuasion and influence, not only will you manage to increase your sales and online presence but it will help you to successfully establish and gain popularity even without monetary investment in the future.

Principles of Persuasion

The different forms of persuasion have been around for a while and based on the principles introduced by Dr. Robert Cialdini. It shows that these persuasion techniques and principles help people to say yes more often when you request something. Applying the principles of persuasion to your social marketing strategies on Facebook can benefit you a great deal and help you to get more responses to your business page. In order to guide human behavior, you need to follow the persuasion principles religiously if you are looking for positive results. Here we will discuss the six principles so you can apply them to your Facebook marketing strategies and achieve success.

Reciprocity

The nature of reciprocation is always handled well when you reciprocate good behavior with a service or a product. People start feeling good and there is an obligation they have towards you. If you go for a party empty-handed you start to feel out of place, which is why every time people invited to a party will turn up with a gift in their hand. Similarly, when you market your business on Facebook you are inviting people to like your Facebook page and interact with you and, in return, you need to reciprocate with small gestures. This could include anything from an offer to a discount. It doesn't need to be something big. Even small gestures can go a long way.

Scarcity

Another great way to persuade people into choosing your business products or services is to create scarcity. This means you need to announce that it's a limited period offer and more people are ordering it, which is why they start thinking it's a great product and this is why everyone wants it. Psychologically, scarcity of products automatically increases the demand, which is why using terms like the last few pieces left in stock or limited offer is something that attracts more people to an advertisement. When using scarcity you have to play with your words wisely to ensure that you don't promote the same product over and over again because that will create doubts in people's minds and they will think that this is a marketing gimmick.

Authority

The next principle of persuasion is an authority and it may sound a bit harsh but it actually works very well to persuade people into doing what you want them to do. However, if you want to make authority work in your favor you have got to have a thorough knowledge of your business and answer any possible questions. It's like giving somebody more information than required that will let them know how credible your business is.

Consistency

This is the fourth principle of persistence and it is one that makes a lot of sense. People always look for consistency when it comes to marketing campaigns. When you achieve consistency in your marketing campaigns you will be able to make sure that you convince people with regards to your business as well as your ideas. There are a number of businesses that look to persuade people without being consistent. Let's say for example you are trying to build your business brand name on Facebook. If you are a business that sells health products and you claim that there are no side-effects, your customer feedback cannot contradict your claims. You need to make sure that your product is consistent with your claims. If you sell products based on a lie, sooner or later your bluff will be caught. You need to make sure that you deliver your campaigns with consistency and you make claims that will hold true even when somebody purchases your product. When you start pursuing people with consistency and you follow up with your claims, you will become a reputable brand in the market because of positive word of mouth publicity.

Liking

This is the fifth principle of appreciation. People will always say yes to something that they like. Not only does this hold true in terms of business but it also holds true in terms of the people that we surround ourselves with. You will always be friends with people that you like and not because you are forced to be with somebody. This is also the case with business. Nobody is going to purchase your product if they do not like you as a brand. This means that your Facebook campaign needs to create a general feeling of liking among people. This is why you need to focus on campaigns that have a feel-good factor and people should be able to connect with the work that you are doing. You will see a number of businesses that go out of their way to help certain communities and give back to society when needed. This is how the principle of liking works. You should know that liking always equals brand loyalty as well as sales.

Consensus

The last principle is the consensus. The consensus is when a group of people look at each other's behavior and then decide upon their own behavior. The principle of consensus simply shows the buyer that the majority of people out there are also doing it. Whether that is true or not is another question altogether. You will see a number of ad campaigns that will claim that 80% of people purchased this product or 50% of people are using a certain product these days. This is enough to convince most of the customers out there that the general consensus is good. This is what is known as going with the flow. When a majority of your customers agree with you, they will try to mimic what the others are doing. If you are a company that sells products that are made of paper and you are trying to convince people to recycle the paper once they have used the product then you need to show that consensus is on your side. The small print on your product stating 75% of your customers recycle this paper when they are done using it goes a long way in convincing others to do it as well. The principle of consensus is extremely powerful and you need to use it to your advantage in order to build a brand name and convince people.

Chapter 2 - The Foundation

The Important Buyer Persona Questions That You Need To Ask

Buyer personas play a huge role in determining the success of a marketing strategy because at the end of the day it is important for you to know as much about your potential buyers as possible so that you can market your products to them more effectively and in a personalized manner. If you are a little bit confused with regards to how you should determine a buyer persona and what filters need to be added in order for the campaign to be a successful one, you need to continue reading. There is so much information out there that it could become intimidating just thinking about what you should and shouldn't include. If you are a small business and you are looking to market on Facebook effectively, here are a few persona questions you should ask in order to identify the audience

Understand Personal Demographics

Demographic information is a great place to begin with because it helps you to narrow down your buyers in an effective way to see whether they fit into the criteria you are looking for. There are many demographics you can include and, apart from location and age, you can also check for demographics that will help you to find the gender, household income, and whether or not they have children or are single or dating.

Educational Background

Understanding the level of education of potential buyers can also help you to figure out whether or not they are ideal buyers for your product. If you are omitting people from a particular University or college, you simply need to ask them the name of their university or college to identify the buyer persona.

Career Path

Some businesses need to target people who hold a certain designation or belong to a certain industry and using this particular buyer persona can help you to narrow down the selection quite easily.

Identifying the Industry of the Buyer Persona

It makes a lot of sense for you to look for people from a certain industry because they may be in a particular employment role that scatters across various industries, and if you want to talk with those people it's difficult to do it by selecting the industry and then narrowing it down to the kind of people you want to talk to. For example, if you are looking for products to sell to a hospital you can't just get in touch with any Human Resource Department. You need to narrow down your industry selection to the hospital and Medical Services only.

The Size of the Company

It is also important for you to know your buyer persona's company. Apart from the Industry, you need details such as the size of the company and the number of employees working for it. If you want to target the entire organization you should always know how many people there are so that you can switch your product accordingly. If you are a B2B business and you are looking to target small and large organizations to sell your product you can always fix the price based on the number of products you would sell and the only way you will be able to determine the number of potential buyers is by the size of the company.

Job Title or Role

Sometimes, someone may be into professional sales and you may or may not be able to determine whether they are the right people or not for the job, and figuring out the job title or role can help you decide whether they are in a position to make a decision or not.

Who Do They Report To?

It's important for you to know who your buyer persona's

report to because if they are not the point of contact to go ahead with your business idea, then there will be somebody above them, and unless you identify that person this will be your dead end.

Information about Their Daily Routine On A Work Day

This question is not relevant to a buyer persona question, but when you know what a particular day looks like, you know exactly when to talk with them or when to place a call where they are less likely to be busy and you will be able to get in touch with them and discuss the business opportunity.

What Tools Do You Use And What Knowledge To You Have?

This question will help you understand what kind of tools your customers use on a daily basis in their job and what level of technical knowledge they have. You need to understand if they use any applications such as Photoshop or a CRM, and how often they use it. This will also give you an idea of the kind of products that they like using and the products that they stay away from. You should try to draw parallels between the products they like and products that you are selling, and this will help you pitch your product appropriately.

What Are Your Challenges?

When you are in a business you need to understand the kind of challenges that people are facing and how you can solve them. With this question, you will try to understand what kind of problems people are facing daily. This will help you to pitch your product accordingly, based on the challenges. For example, you are a company that makes earphones. If your customer is a transcriber and he or she states that they are not able to hear their audio very well because of the background noise, you can pitch your product stating that you have noise-cancellation software that can help them focus on your audio and transcribe better. This is just a small example and there are other parallels that you can draw based on the customer's problems and the solution that you are offering.

What Kind Of Work Are You Responsible For?

This question will help you to understand the persona of your potential buyers and see the level of stress that they are under. You can also try to help your customers achieve their goals or overcome the challenges based on this question. If you sell electronic appliances and a customer states that they get late when they are trying to get things done in the morning, you can then pitch your products, such as a toaster that is quicker than others or an alarm clock that is really effective in waking you up.

Where Do You Get Your Information From/Which Websites Of Blogs Do You Frequently Visit?

In order to understand your buyer, you need to make sure that you look at their internet usage and how they use the internet to their advantage. This question will help you understand their social network usage, as well as their usage of search engines. You will also understand which sources they trust and how often they read blogs online. If you find that most of your customers refer to blogs for information then you can start your own business blog and get them to subscribe to it. Blogs are the best way to gain the confidence of customers and build a brand name without being too obvious about it.

Where Do You Purchase Your Products From?

This will help you understand what kind of online shopping activities your customers do. If most of your customers are comfortable shopping online then you need to create the ideal sales experience for them. You need to get into their comfort zone so that you can reciprocate their sales experience and help build your brand name.

A Basic Buy Persona Template Example

Age	
Location	
Language	
Job title	
Average income	
Buying behavior	

Interests & activities	
Life stage	

Pain Points and Goals

Customer pain point	Customer goal	How you can help?
[**Example**: We have trouble keeping our fans on social media engagement because we only have so much time to dedicate to each network.]	[**Example**: We want to be able to engage our social media audience and save time.]	[**Example**: Your business allows you to schedule posts and messages across networks from a single dashboard.]

Pain point #2	Goal #2	Your solution #2
Pain point #3	Goal #3	Your solution #3
Pain point #4	Goal #4	Your solution #4

Real Estate Example

Age	30 Years

Location	New York
Language	English
Job title	Software Engineer
Average income	$150000
Buying behavior	First Time Buyer
Interests & activities	Computers, Swimming, Music
Life stage	Single

Pain Points and Goals

Customer pain point	Customer goal	How your product/business can help?
No time to go house hunting	Find the ideal house and close on escrow	Give a virtual tour
Budget constraints	Find house within budget with wiggle room for renovations / minor interior changes	Look for a smaller, cozy home - or ready to move in home that requires no additional expenses.

Restaurant Example

Age	45 years

Location	Dallas
Language	English
Job title	Homemaker
Average income	$50000
Buying behavior	Return customer
Interests & activities	Socializing, partying, kid-friendly activities
Life stage	Married, with two kids.

Pain Points and Goals

Customer pain point	Customer goal	How your business/product can help?
Looking to celebrate the kid's birthday party	Needs a place big enough to accommodate 100 guests (Budget constraints)	Offer package deals with mini-meals and fun kid activities and a parent area to socialize

Chapter 3: Start Growing Your Business with Facebook

Although Facebook was under the scanner in 2018 for not maintaining data transparency, it still happens to be the number one platform for people to socialize on a regular basis. This is a considerable amount of people who like keeping themselves updated with what's happening in and around them but scrolling through what was initially called the Facebook wall. If you are a small business owner there is no denying that Facebook is the best way for you to market your business and help it to grow fast.

What Content Can You Create On Facebook

Facebook has a wide range of different tools that small businesses can benefit from. Whether you choose to use it organically or through various methods, you can definitely benefit by creating a Facebook page and using it to your advantage. Organic content that you share on your Facebook page starts gaining more and more popularity if you combine it with ad campaigns that you plan strategically.

There are various campaigns you can conduct on Facebook, and whether you choose pictures, carousel, or video format, you can increase the online presence of your business to a great extent. You can also consider using blogs and video content to initiate conversation or follow it at a later stage.

How to Effectively Market With Facebook

If you choose a Facebook business manager to begin your campaign, you can use multiple filters to set your goal and create awareness or increase the sales of your product effectively. Facebook has some interesting tools that not only help you to target people more practically but also in a more systematic manner, which means you will not spend money on unnecessary lead generation. Genetic exposure is not effective because this is not going to get you any revenue or help your business grow. If you want your business to succeed you need Facebook marketing to work in your favor. You need to use it to target the right customers and that's where your buyer persona and the effective tools that Facebook have to help segregate the audience come in handy.

Facebook Marketing Advantages

While Facebook may look very simple from the onset, it does provide a lot of creative support and helps small businesses grow their brand name. Facebook provides you with a lot of tools that will help you create content for your desktop as well as mobile devices. Even if you have no designing skills, you will be able to create content for your small business with the help of Facebook. Some of the content that you can create on Facebook includes:

Images

There are a number of images that you can create on Facebook with the help of the creator support that is available behind the scenes. It has been seen that any post that has images will get more engagement than a text-only post. There are a number of resources that will help you to create images using clipart as well as photo resources. You will be able to brand your image and put your point across with the help of this resource.

Video Content

Video content has a massive reach, however, very few businesses use video to their advantage. A video could be anything related to your business such as an advertisement or even a campaign that shows your business in a good light. There are a number of video creation options that Facebook has and you should use this to your advantage in order to help your business prosper.

Live Facebook

This is another great tool that Facebook provides to all of its users. As a small business, it is very beneficial to use Facebook live and interact with your customers in real-time. You will be able to get an instant reaction and you will see your business prosper.

Facebook also offers targeting opportunities for small businesses. You will be able to target specific customers based on their behavior. Behavioral targeting not only helps you reach the right audience, but it will also help create an impact in no time. This targeting feature helps you target local communities as well as large geographical areas. This feature is extremely important because in today's world, targeting random people for promoting a business is not going to work in your favor.

Paid Content Vs Organic Content

Over the years Facebook has been known to encourage organic content, however, that trend changed a couple of years ago. Facebook started paid advertising and started downgrading organic content. This caused a number of businesses opting in for paid content because organic content reached very few potential customers. Facebook was no longer happy with just regular posts and updates in the organic news feed. Going with the paid option was one of the best things to do if you wanted to get noticed on Facebook.

However, recently Facebook changed its approach and began returning to its roots. In 2018 it started favoring personal content over promotional content. Facebook has also started appreciating content that is shareable, valuable, and community-based. You no longer need to rely on corporate methods of promotion. You only need to create content that will fit into your customer's newsfeed. Facebook customers now have the option of marking certain advertisements as spam and if you do not want your ads to be listed as spam you need to start getting organic with your content and get more personal with your customers.

Creating A Facebook Business Account

Setting up a business page is extremely important to make sure that your business has some kind of identity on Facebook. Facebook offers a number of tools to small businesses to promote their products and services and this can be done with the help of the business manager. The business manager allows you to create your Facebook page, identify your audience, and list down your product catalog. You can even set up permissions for your account and give the user access to various employees on your page as well as your apps. The business manager will even allow you to track your advertisements and see the kind of impressions you are making and how much you are spending on your ads.

Creating Your Account

When creating your account you need to go to business.Facebook.com/create and click on the option to create an account. Then you need to enter your name and enter your Facebook login credentials. You will then get several prompts that you need to follow in order to create your business account. Once you have entered all the information you then need to go ahead and select the settings and assign permissions to your Facebook account. You can assign up to two people as your administrator and these are the people that will approve posts and they will be responsible for maintaining the page. You don't need to add a new ad account. This account will help manage all your advertisements and make sure that you tweak the ads based on your requirements.

Assigning Levels

Once you have created your business account and you have given permissions, you then need to assign levels to the people that are on your team. You need to decide roles for your employees and these rules will hold true across all accounts, the business app, as well as the ad account.

Add a Payment Method

When you set up your business account you also need to add a payment method. This payment method will allow you to pay for Facebook ads and also receive a line of credit whenever you are eligible. You will need to define a payment method before you create your ad account.

Creating a Facebook Company Fan Page

Every business needs a fan page in order to grow their business and get the word out there. Just creating a Facebook account is not sufficient. You need a fan page to interact with your fans and make sure that you generate sufficient leads and increase sales for your business. Here are a few simple steps that will show you how to create your business fan page and generate leads and interact with your potential customers.

You need to first go to Facebook.com/pages. Once you are on the website then you need to click on the 'create a page' button that appears on the upper right-hand side of the page. Then you will be asked to select the category for your business. This could be a local business, an organization, a company, an artist, a brand, a public figure, a community, or entertainment. If you are not sure which category your business falls under then you could either select company, organization, or institution.

Once you have decided which category your business belongs to, you will then be asked to fill out information regarding the business. Depending on the category that you selected you will be given subcategories to choose from and then you will need to enter your company name. You will then need to select that you agree with the Facebook page terms and click the 'get started' button.

Enter Basic Information

The next stage is entering the information for your business and uploading a profile picture. You will also be asked to select a Facebook web address and fill in the 'about' section. When you are uploading the profile picture for your business you should pick an image that is 180 pixels by 180 pixels. When you have uploaded this image it will show on your fan page. After you upload the picture you need to click on the button that says 'save photo' and then click next. If you do not have a picture ready to upload you can even skip this step for now.

When filling out the basic information for your business you need to enter information that is clear and accurate. You should also include keywords that are relevant to your business as this will help with the SEO of the business page. You then need to type in your website URL and set up your Facebook link. You need to make this link short as well as memorable because this is the link that your potential customers will use to find you. If your business name is very difficult to remember you need to consider using something shorter that will be easy to recollect.

Use the Admin Panel

When you become a fan page administrator you will be able to see the admin panel. This admin panel will give you information regarding your pages, such as new people that have recently liked your page, notifications regarding your page post, and information regarding how your fan page is performing. You can use the control panel to add new administrators and you can even edit the information on your fan page. You can invite people to like your page and follow it, however, you need to be careful about using this option because if your pages are empty people may not want to follow your page. Put relevant information regarding your business and add content to make people interested in following you.

Tell Stories

People do not like random posts that are put up on fan pages. Your content will decide how successful your fan page is and this is what you need to focus on. It is important to share regular status updates, milestones, and images along with videos that will tell a story to the audience. All your updates on your fan page should revolve around your brand as this will help create an impact amongst your fans.

Build Tabs to Generate Sales

You need to then build tabs on your fan page that will help connect with your leads and increase traffic to your website. You can create one tab that will help you get email ids while another tab will help sell your products. Facebook even allows you to accept payments through its integrated payment gateway. Your fan page can promote and sell your business on its own as long as the content is relevant and interesting.

Facebook Marketing Tips for Small Businesses

Facebook is focusing on delivering content that is useful to users and, in most cases, organic content is declining. If you are spending to advertise on Facebook for your small business, it is necessary for you to make the right decision in order for the marketing efforts to pay off.

It's common for small businesses to lower marketing expenses on Facebook because of not being too sure whether or not they will be able to choose the right path. There's nothing to worry about because no matter how limited your budget is, a little persuasion and the right influencer will manage to get more customers for your business.

Post with Intent

You have to think about what you want to share on Facebook and how you would like to interact with your audience. Reciprocation is necessary which is why you have got to focus on content that establishes two-way communication rather than just being a platform for you to share without knowing whether or not it's actually interesting to your customers. The more people reciprocate, the higher the chances of the content going viral, and you will benefit from it.

Try To Blend In

Your Facebook marketing tactics don't have to stand out in your campaigns. It needs to be subtle but clear, so people know what you're talking about but they also enjoy the content you share. Whether it's a humorous post something informative to make sure that anyone who checks your post benefits from it even if you don't benefit from them.

Don't Forget Your Content Calendar

A content calendar helps you to effectively plan your posts and schedule them even on days you won't be accessing your computer, and this helps regular interaction and posting, which is vital for your Facebook page and your marketing efforts to work.

Optimize Your Profile Page

Your Facebook business page is the face of your business and has to be complete. Make sure all the information is updated on the page; that will make it easy for the customer to get in touch with you. Whether it is providing the timings of your business operations or giving them the official website to visit always make sure information on your Facebook business page is updated.

Clear the Community Page

A smart way to use persuasion principles in Facebook marketing is by creating a community page. You can not only manage to make people feel special and reciprocate but you can also create an illusion of scarcity of products or services that they automatically want to invest in.

Create a Facebook Group

It's difficult to handle so many Facebook accounts. You need to make sure you share the right kind of information on the right pages. The benefit of creating a group is that you can invite people to like it, and this is a subtle persuasion principle that you can put to use and benefit from. One of the best things about creating a Facebook group is that you can automatically increase your likes without spending money by simply inviting your circle of friends and family members to join in.

Strategically Choose Your Name

Sometimes your business name might already be taken up by another Facebook page and this may get you extremely disappointed. If you are a local business, try using your business name and local city name to let people know the difference between your Facebook page and the other one.

Use the Facebook story to your advantage

People are always curious to watch your Facebook story because it goes away after 24 hours. This will give people the curiosity to see what's happening and it helps you increase visibility on Facebook.

Start With One Advertisement At A Time On A Limited Budget

When you start advertising on Facebook, always begin with a small budget. Even if you fail, you know for a fact that you didn't invest too much money and it gives you the motivation to start over.

Consider Boosting Posts

When you share something organically and you realize it is doing really well, consider boosting the post to get more exposure. This can be done with a small budget and it can give you the kind of revenue returns you were seeking.

You can also try to use Facebook pixel and other add-on tools to your benefit one at a time to see which works well for you. Most Facebook marketing strategies can be applied to other social media platforms as well, as long as you use them effectively. While it's good to have a social media presence across all platforms, it is important for you to focus on one at a time so that you create a strong influence on one platform before you move to the other.

Biggest mistakes you make on Your Facebook Profile & Fan Page

It is important for you to understand the various mistakes people usually make when it comes to promoting their business on Facebook. This helps to avoid making these silly mistakes that will cost you the right kind of exposure and limit your marketing efforts.

Posting too many times on Facebook

Whether it's sharing on your private business page or fan page, you need to make sure that you limit the number of posts to a maximum of 5 posts a day for businesses. Posting irrelevant information too many times is not going to help your Facebook page. Some business owners are in the habit of sharing too much information from other pages thinking that it will benefit them and help them to get more exposure. This is not beneficial for your business in any way, so make sure you focus on sharing information relevant to your business at the right time.

Not Engaging In Comments

It is vital for business owners to have two-way communication and reciprocate with potential customers and existing customers if you want persuasion to continue. The best way to do this is to engage in the comments whether good, bad, or ugly and reply to your customers regularly.

Arguing

One of the worst things you can do is arguing with people on your Facebook page because this will create a negative impact and hamper the reputation of your business. Always leave positive feedback, irrespective of how hurtful comment is.

Deleting negative comments

It's not recommended to delete comments unless they have pornographic or graphic content. If something is said to you or your business, try dealing with it but do not delete a negative comment against your business; rather, show a brave face to prove credibility.

Running competitions against the rules

Running a competition on Facebook and trying to lure customers by promising them a gift when you don't actually provide them with one is something you should avoid doing. Facebook does not share information directly with business owners and if a business owner wants to get in touch with the customer they need to do it directly.

Posting similar content

Maintaining a business page is extremely difficult if you are not sure what you need to update on it. Some businesses update just one type of content on a daily basis. This content is usually in the form of images that give out a social message or promote the brand name. While posting images is fine, doing the same thing multiple times a day can get monotonous, and your fans will lose interest in your page. You need to post things that add value to your business page and also show your fans that you are interested in communicating with them. Try to make some interactions by asking for the opinions by inviting them to certain sales. This will make fans want to look forward to your next post and it will also help improve your brand value. You can always mix things up by putting up a joke or putting a funny message, but these are the things that should not dominate your fan page. Your fan page should be about your fans and your business and nothing else.

Not using applications properly

There are a number of built-in applications on Facebook that help you create campaigns and drive more traffic to your business. Most fan pages do not use this to their advantage and they end up hoping fans will turn up to their business website and get converted into a sale. You cannot live on hope in the world of business. You need to take the initiative and use the applications as well as the tabs to your advantage. Introduce competitions amongst the fans and create various campaigns that will help promote your business. When fans start showing interest in your business and they stand to gain something out of it, it will work wonders for your popularity.

Not responding

Social media is all about interaction with fans and when the interaction stops, you will end up losing a lot of followers. Most fans usually comment positively on your posts and you should make it a point to reply to these comments. If there are too many comments you can always thank them in your next post rather thanking them individually. If there is a negative comment or if somebody is asking a specific question, make sure you individually respond to such comments because this will put you in good light and it will show the fans that you are interested in communicating with them. The key to responding is doing it fast. Replying after two days to a comment is not going to be helpful.

Generating traffic to your website

The purpose of a fan page should be to increase traffic to your website. This can be done in a number of ways and with various calls to action. You need to mix up your call to action and persuade your audience by using the six principles of persuasion. These principles are proven and you should be able to increase traffic to your website in no time. Mix up your content and make sure that the fans do not get bored with what you are offering. Asking your fans to visit your website through each and every post is not going to do the trick because fans eventually realize that your intention is wrong.

The Most Common Persuasion Mistakes

Using the rules of persuasion to lure people into showing interest in your business is a common habit most small business owners adapt to. Principles work really well in helping your business get the kind of exposure that it needs. It's important to understand how to avoid the common mistakes people make when they try to use these principles for marketing.

Validating undesirable

Too many times people share stuff on social media that may not necessarily be accepted. With a view to reciprocate to that post a lot of business owners go to validate the behavior. You need to understand that you have got to stay away from such posts, even though you may want to reciprocate because it's not healthy to confuse contacts with reciprocity.

Just because somebody purchases a product from you doesn't necessarily mean you have to return the favor by doing something in addition to providing them with the product. When it comes to marketing business your reciprocation is in the form of quality products or services you provide and you need to focus on that rather than giving an additional service or product that has no value or meaning in the life of the customer. Sometimes it's always better to stay away and be a silent spectator. If these comments are on your Facebook page you can always reciprocate in a healthy manner without validating the behavior.

Highlight gain instead of the loss

Many times business owners tend to spend more money on promoting their business than they actually get a profit out of. One of the major reasons we need to start with small marketing efforts is because it helps to understand just how profitable the entire strategy or plan is. When it doesn't work out you can always change the strategy to something more effective but when you invest too much time and money in one particular plan and focus on the few profits instead of focusing on the major losses your business does not grow.

Misusing your authority

The principle of authority is one principle that a lot of businesses misuse. People usually look at influencers in social media when they make their decisions. These influencers help customers make decisions based on their personal experiences as well as the facts. Some of these influencers end up misusing the authority and give wrong information to the customers. You need to make sure you do not repeat these mistakes because when you misuse the principle of authority and the trust is broken, customers will not hesitate before they speak out. Rather than convincing somebody that your product is good, even though it has flaws, you need to make sure that you work on the flaws and improve your product before asking customers to opt for it.

The principle of liking

You need to build your relationship based on this principle. Most businesses are very happy with a few likes on your Facebook and are content without following up on those likes. If a follower likes any of your content, you need to make sure that you connect further with them and make sure that they converted into a customer. If you do not see too many likes coming on your Facebook fan page then you should try to make customers like you rather than forcing them to like your posts. Posting over and over again is not going to gain you any additional customers. You need to speak about your brand and make people like you because the principle of liking is very strong. Once customers start liking you they will always look forward to your posts and they will stay loyal to your business.

Enforcing the principle of consistency

Most businesses fall flat with this principle because they are not sure how to bring about consistency in their behavior. Changing a few statements and posts can bring about a change as long as it stays consistent with your brand image. If you are promoting ethical behavior then your post should also reflect that behavior. When you start contradicting this principle, you will see your number of followers backing down.

Not giving a reason

When you do not provide a reason for a certain kind of behavior you will not gain the trust of your customers. If the pricing for any of your products has increased you need to explain to your customers through your fan page for the reason in the increase. Doing things without reason will not work in your favor because customers want to know why they are being affected because of a change in your policies.

Proven Ways to Boost Organic (Non-Paid) Facebook Posts

Facebook uses an algorithm to determine which posts of yours are popular and which are not. Posts that have the potential to go viral can always be boosted and these posts can not only manage to help you get more exposure but they can market your business without any expense. Here are some smart ways to boost your Facebook marketing efforts without spending any money.

Analyze Your Top 10

One of the best ways to post on Facebook and know it will get exposure is to check in on your Facebook marketing efforts and see the most popular posts that you shared in the form of advertisements. Select those posts and use them in a persuasive manner to promote it again but in an organic way.

Post amazing content

In order for a business to post healthy content, they need to make sure that they follow the Persuasion principles because this method pretty much guarantees more followers and it's important for you to have responsive posts if you want your business to stay popular on Facebook. Take time to create the content or hire a specialist to do this, but make sure that all the content you post is good quality and the kind of sentences people look forward to seeing.

Optimize targeting

You can filter the kind of people you want to target on Facebook, so do that by applying a variety of filters to the post that can help you get better exposure to people that matter most.

Don't cross-post

The posters on Twitter have no relevance on Facebook and hashtags are not trending right now, so you need to make sure that you design posts specifically for each platform and share it on those platforms only.

Learn the best times to post

There's a lot of information out there with regards to which is the best for you to share on Facebook, but the best way to figure that out is to see what time your previous posts got the best response and mimic those steps taken to posting at that time.

Share on weekends as well

It's important for you to share information on weekends, and in case you not planning to go to your office, you can always use scheduling tools like Hootsuite to automatically send outposts on weekends to engage customers and potential customers.

Make the most of Facebook live

Facebook live is an amazing feature that will allow you to communicate directly with your customers. You can stream any events you're hosting or even celebrations within your organization. A number of small businesses provide updates to their customers through the Facebook live feature. If you are a real estate business, you can provide live views to a new listing in your portfolio. Not only does this get you more outreach, but it will also help customers communicate and connect with you in a better manner.

Use your blog posts to your advantage

A number of businesses run blog posts simultaneously and this is something that you should also get into the habit of doing. Your blog posts are a great way to communicate with your customers, and getting customers to your blog is not an easy task. You can start embedding your blog URL into your Facebook content, which helps redirect customers to your blog when they click on your images or posts to increase views on your blog. If you have an onsite blog, this automatically increases traffic to your website which contributes to SEO efforts in the long run.

Use events to your advantage

Creating an event on Facebook does not cost you anything and it can give you the outreach that you desire. When you announce a sale or an upcoming launch via an event, people will start showing interest because they have nothing to lose. Even if you get a 10% conversion from the number of people that attend your event, your event can be termed as successful.

Make use of webinars

A number of businesses use webinars to communicate with customers as well as employees across the world. You can now use Facebook as a webinar discussion board and invite people to join the discussion. When a lot of people start joining a webinar it will automatically boost your Facebook page and you will reach more customers.

Email marketing

You need to use your Facebook fan page to collect emails from potential customers. You need to then use these email ids and utilize them in your email marketing campaigns. Since most of the recipients will know your business they will not mark emails as spam and they may end up liking your business and promote your business to their family members and friends. Email marketing has a lot of scopes and you can use it in collaboration with Facebook marketing to get good results.

Using Pinterest

If your products or services are appealing to women you need to make sure that you use Pinterest to your advantage as well. Most small businesses upload the Facebook images on Pinterest as well and backlink it to the fan page. This strategy has worked tremendously and a number of businesses have seen an increase in their followers.

Ask your fans to enable notifications

While you may have over a million followers on your Facebook page, not all of them will know if you have posted something new. This could be because they are not following you and your updates will not appear in their news feed. You can ask people to follow your notifications as well so that they get an update and your followers on your fan page will convert into potential customers.

Facebook Engagement Tactics for Your Business Page

The first principle of persuasion is reciprocating, which means it's important for you to interact with your potential customers and customers if you want your business to grow and get the kind of exposure you believe it deserves. There are different things you can do on Facebook if you want to engage with your customers but you have to come up with effective ways you can convince people to reciprocate.

Collect questions in comments

Always encourage your audience to reply to questions about your business, asking for suggestions, put them in the spotlight and tell them to give you certain tips and tricks on how you can either improve what they are looking forward to from your business. Not only does this help you to interact with your potential customers and customers, it lets you know what they are looking for and you to strive to be a more customer-oriented business.

Share offers about products to anyone who pings you on messenger

This is a unique and smart way to get people to reciprocate. All you need to do is have a small code ready that you can share with them on messenger every time they ping you. This will also help give you an idea of how many people are actually watching your business and what kind of reaction they have to the posts that you shared.

Use emojis to your advantage

People love looking at emojis and it shows that you have a friendly and casual approach in your business, which makes it easier for people to communicate with you. These emojis are easy to use and they help spread a more sentimental message that helps you connect with the people.

Shout out to customers

When someone purchases something from your business or you have a new customer that you are proud of, have a shout out and let them know that you are feeling appreciated and loved. However, when you plan on doing this make sure that you ask the customer for permission prior to creating the post just to make sure you don't make the customer feel embarrassed or out of place.

Run a contest!

Post a riddle on Facebook and ask people to answer it. Give them a gift voucher or a chance to win something big if they reply with the right answer. This is a lot of potential reaches and many customers love engaging, not just because of the prize but because they want to test their intellectual skills.

Ask for feedback

Customers usually love when they are included in any decision-making, and this is what you should be doing with your Facebook posts. A number of businesses have to interact with the customers in this manner and have tried to get their views on certain business decisions. Not only does this help with increased engagement, but it also ensures that fans look forward to contributing to your business success. This can be done in the form of a survey or asking a question on a Facebook fan page and noting down the answers. You should also reply to the feedback on your fan page and let people know you appreciate their suggestions.

Share relevant information

Most of the time you do not need to share information regarding your business. You need to make sure that you share information that will be helpful to customers because this will create a positive impact on their minds. If you are in the health business then you can share information regarding an outbreak of a virus that people need to be careful about. This does not necessarily promote your brand but it will show people that you care about them even if they are not your customers yet.

Ask open-ended questions

Try to have a bit of fun with your audience and ask them questions that they will love answering and will be beneficial to your business as well. For example, if you are in the hotel business you can ask questions such as 'how much are you willing to pay for a fancy meal with your significant better half?'. People will love answering this question and they will even give you vital information with regards to what people's budget is. Once you have collated all the information, make sure that you launch an event or offer something to the customers in return that will connect back with your question. In this example, you can offer a one-time-only dinner for two for $200, if that is the amount that most people have said they would pay for a romantic dinner date.

Start Joining Conversations That Are Relevant

Look at the world around you and create the content that will be relevant to what's happening across borders. You need to start aligning your posts with news and give information to people because world news will affect them. Try being a friend to your audience rather than a salesperson. You will see the level of interaction increasing when you start posting relevant information on your fan page.

Speak About Your Community Involvement

People love it when businesses give back to society and you need to make sure that you do that as well. While most people would not know what you have done to help society, you could provide information to the people proactively and show them that you care and are giving back when it's needed the most. If your local area has been hit by a flood, you can give out free food to all the people that are homeless or are struggling. This gesture will definitely pay off and your fans will be grateful when you do something for others.

Don't be serious all the time

Add a bit of humor to your posts every now and then because everyone needs a laugh occasionally. Do not try to put others down with your jokes and also try to stay away from political statements or religious statements. Generic humor will be accepted by a majority of your audience and you will not have to regret putting any of this up.

Examples of Interactive Facebook Posts

Type Of Posts	Example 1 (Realtor - Local Business)	Example 2 (Restaurant - Local Business)
Contest	Tell us what you think about the latest bridge construction in one word	Give us your famous 3-Ingredient recipe!
Run A Poll Or A Survey	What's better? Oceanview or Gardenview? Share your opinion with	Have you tried out our new desserts yet? Tell us which

	us now	one you'd like to continue seeing on the menu!
Facebook Live	New open house today for all via Facebook Live. Get a virtual tour! Click on the link to book your slot.	Watch our cook live in action as he prepares his famous Chilli Chicken recipe! Watch and learn!
Create Events	Ten new open houses scheduled in the Dallas area next week. Click if you are interested and invite your friends along as well.	We're finally opened for wedding bookings! Booking from Monday - Check the listing on our fan page!
Share Inspirational Stories	See how this 24-year old built an ultimate dream home for his parents! Get those tissues out!	Watch this war veteran propose to his fiancee over a romantic dinner! There is nothing better

		that you'll see on the internet today!

Scroll Stopping Content

When you market on Facebook you need to make sure that you create content that stops people from scrolling and make them want to take a look at whatever you have to share. You have a very small window to influence people to do that before they scroll past your post, so you need to make sure you include bright vibrant pictures and catchy phrases that don't take too long for a person to read. Video content works really well as long as there is a catchy tagline to it.

A major mistake people make when sharing video content is not adding a tagline. People are not going to guess the video content and they will not watch it unless there's something that makes them curious or tugs on an emotional string. When you put the principles of persuasion along with the right tactics Facebook marketing, you manage to come up with a scroll-stopping post that will benefit your business.

Why do people share content?

A Facebook advertisement is usually a place to share

information. People are not really sure what they need to share and what they should stay away from. Most people will share when it elicits a positive response in their mind. Happy posts are something that a lot of people will openly share. Another post people usually tend to share is information regarding health or maybe a post that has gone viral. The trick to making people want to share a post is to engage with them. The more engaging or interesting your posts, the more people will want to share it and make others aware of it. As a business owner, you need to keep the following points in mind when it comes to sharing habits.

- almost 60% of people share a post when they find it interesting and relevant to their daily lives.
- 40% of the posts are shared are because people found that the content was funny.
- 30% of posts were shared because it was a social message and people believed in that message.
- 35% of people share posts when they found that it was regarding a sales recommendation. For example posts regarding the 10 best smartphones that cost less than $100.
- 25% of posts were shared when they were promoting a social cause or promoting a local business.

You need to understand the psychology of your readers in order to make your post shareable.

Targeting on Facebook

Sharing information without a target audience on Facebook is not going to benefit your business in any way because unless you talk with customers who are relevant to your business you are not going to make any money. If you are a local business and somebody who is not local sees your advertisement, it's not going to do much for you as a business owner. It's important for you to understand the various ways you can target customers by using filters on Facebook to narrow down people who are most likely potential customers or will be interested in your business.

Targeting on Facebook can be done in a number of ways. You need to look at all the criteria which could be relevant to your customers and target based on these criteria. Some of the criteria include:

Location

If you want your business to grow locally then you should target customers that are local. If you do not have the capacity to scale at the national or international level then there is no point selecting customers from different geographic areas.

Demographics

You need to get the demographics right when it comes to targeting the right audience. Most products and services would be relevant to a certain age group or even certain sex. You need to also target specific demographics such as marital status as well as yearly earnings.

Interest

Most customers update their interest on their Facebook page. You need to use this to your advantage and target people based on the interests they have mentioned. If you are a company that promotes music then you can sell jazz music to people who love that genre.

Look for partner connections

Partner connections are important because you will be able to target an audience before anyone else as targets them. For example, if you are looking to sell a new smartphone, look for customers that have contacted a local repair shop. If a customer's phone is not working, there is a 50% chance that they may look for a new smartphone in the near future.

Chapter 4: How to Set up Facebook Business Manager

A lot of people tend to avoid using Facebook business manager because they believe that it is a complicated setup that will consume a lot of their time. One of the best things about the Facebook business manager is it actually helps you to save on a lot of time and, while the initial setup may seem complicated, once you've gone through it, you will be able to benefit from it long-term. Here is a detailed break-up of how you can set up your Facebook business manager by following the simple steps.

Create Your Facebook Business Manager Account

In order for you to create your Facebook business manager, you need to first create an account. In order for you to do this, you have got to go to business.Facebook.com and click on the create account big blue button which is at the left of the top of the screen. You then need to fill out all your information in the popup box and continue. Make sure that you enter your business email address to manage your business account and click finish once all these details are completed.

Add Your Business Page

This is really simple, and if you already have an existing Facebook page, you can automatically integrate it into your Facebook business page with a few steps. If you are trying to replicate your pages, you will need to grant access from your Facebook account to the business manager account in order for this to happen.

In order for you to do this, you need to go to the dashboard, click on the add page, and click add page in the popup box again. If you have more than one account then make sure that you select the right one.

Add Your Facebook Ad Account

Once you get access to the existing Facebook page you can then request access to your Facebook ad account as well, which means if you have existing advertisements, you can control them using the business manager. On the business manager dashboard, once you click on add ad account you will also manage to get access to your ads manager. If you don't have an ad account on Facebook you can then create one in the business manager. In order for you to set up an ad account, you have got to go back to the dashboard, click on the add ad account, and start creating your ad account. You need to enter all your details including an email address, payment method, and a little more information before the account is successfully set up.

Add People to Help Manage the Facebook Business Page

Marketing on Facebook is quite difficult, and if you are a large organization and have multiple tasks at hand you can always hire a business manager to handle the page for you. You can add team members and also limit or restrict the amount of accessibility you want to give to them. There is a people and assets column in the business setting that you need to go to where you can assign assets to certain people and also grant how much access you would like them to have on the manager page itself.

Assign People to Manage Your Facebook Page

There are a number of assets that you would have on Facebook, and you need to be on top of your marketing efforts in order to be successful. In order to be in control of your Facebook marketing efforts, you need to add team members that can help take care of your Facebook business page and control your Facebook ad campaigns. This can be done through the business manager dashboard. When you are on the dashboard you need to click on business settings at the top of the page and then click on the people and assets tab. Under this tab, you need to select people and this will show you a list of people that can access your Facebook business manager. If you have not added anybody then you will only see your name and the address list. You can then start adding team members and assign privileges to each of the team members. You can add a number of people depending on their responsibility. This includes freelance writers, employees, and business partners. This step only involves adding individuals to your Facebook business account. Once you have set the privileges for each of the team members, you then need to click on add people and move to the next section.

Next, you need to decide which of your team members have access to which part of the business page. Some people would have access only to the advertising page while others will have complete control as a moderator. Once you have assigned responsibilities to them, each of your team members will receive an email regarding the same. They need to accept the invitation in order to become a part of the Facebook business page. You need to inform your team members in advance that they could receive an email and they should accept the invitation immediately.

Link to Your Instagram Account

Instagram is an important social media channel and linking it to your Facebook account will give you more outreach. This can be done again under the people and assets tab and then you need to click on add Instagram account. You will then be asked to enter the credentials for your Instagram account. Once you enter that information you need to click next. The next steps will ask you if you have more than one account for your business and you can enter that account information as well.

Now that you have your business manager running, you need to access your dashboard where you can control all the activities for your Facebook business page. Apart from doing the above you also need to go ahead and set up Facebook pixels that will allow you to take your Facebook advertisement to the next level.

Setting Up Facebook Pixels

Facebook pixels is coding that Facebook will help generate for you. When you enter this code on your website it will give access to information such as optimizing Facebook ads and tracking conversion through your website. Facebook pixels is very helpful and it should be set up even before you start your first ad campaign. Under the people and assets tab, you need to select pixels and then click on add. You don't need to give a name for your Facebook pixel account and click on create. On the next page, you have the option of setting up your pixel now and once you click on next, your pixel will be generated. You can create up to 10 pixels for your account and you can use this to your advantage.

Placing Your Ad

When you are on the Facebook business manager dashboard you need to click on business manager that is at the top left-hand side. When you click that, you need to click on create and manage and click on the create button. If you are doing this for the first time, you can select guided creation which will help you set up your campaign objective as well as select your target audience and your budget. Here you will be able to select your schedule for your ads and, when you click on save, you are ready for your first ad to go live. When you follow all the steps correctly you will be set to start your Facebook marketing campaign today.

Reasons You Should Be Advertising on Facebook

There is no denying that social media is definitely ruling the market when it comes to promoting your business online which is why it is very important for you to select the right platform for your business to grow. Facebook is still the best social media platform you can select because it has the highest number of active users and people tend to check Facebook on a regular basis. If you decide that you want to go with social media marketing but you are not too sure why Facebook is the best then here are some things about Facebook advertising you should know about.

Your Audience Is On Facebook

There is no denying that the people who you want to target are available on Facebook and it's easy for you to touch base with them because you are able to easily filter out unnecessary people and limit your budget effectively.

Facebook Advertisements Are Cheaper

There is no denying that Facebook advertising is relatively cheaper in comparison to the other advertising platforms on social media. You can also use organic boosts to increase your fan base and customer reach, which helps you to generate customers without spending any money.

Facebook Targeting Capabilities

There are a number of advertising channels that you can target, however, Facebook targeting is definitely the best. Facebook has a number of targeting capabilities and it includes demographics, interests, behavior, age range, connections, and locations. Each of these capabilities can be further expanded and you will be able to target a specific group with the help of Facebook.

Facebook Helps Convert Leads

Facebook is perfect when it comes to targeting customers that have already visited your website in the past. Irrespective of whether or not these leads became customers in the past, Facebook will keep remarketing to them based on their behavior online. A number of businesses have called this the social stalker. Facebook is capable of stalking all your potential leads and targeting them based on what they currently require. For example, if a customer has been searching for laptops, Facebook will know about this and will promote your business if you are in the laptop business. Facebook will never promote your ad to a customer that has been looking for products that do not fall within your niche.

Get New Leads Easily

Facebook is the perfect platform where you will be able to generate new leads almost on a daily basis. Apart from being able to generate new leads, you can even clone these leads with a lookalike audience feature that Facebook has. This feature enables Facebook to target an audience that is similar to your current target audience but may vary on a couple of parameters. The likelihood of these people also being interested in your business is very high and this is something that only Facebook can do for you. Facebook's target lookalike audience is based on people that have downloaded apps similar to your business app.

Benefits of the Facebook Pixel

Facebook pixel is one of the most interesting add-on tools that Facebook gives you. It's essential to help you create an interesting and successful marketing strategy that works in your favor. If you haven't already started using Facebook pixel then here are a few reasons why it needs to be integrated into your advertisement today.

Understanding Your Audience Better

Facebook pixel provides you with detailed insight that helps you to determine who your existing customers are as well as who are the potential customers. It provides you with analytics that not only identifies the browsing activity of people but also their purchasing activity.

Relevant Engagement

If you are in the e-commerce business and you are looking to talk with people who are relevant to your business using pixel is highly recommended. It uses behavioral targeting to identify people who are looking for services or businesses like yours so that you can get in touch with them faster or they can get in touch with you after they see your advertisement.

Identify Shopping Journeys

The Facebook pixel will help you understand shoppers that

take a long time when they are browsing through products. Pixel data will help you understand what each of the customers looks for when they are selecting a product and what is the one aspect that appeals to them before they make the purchase. For example, for customers shopping for a new pair of jeans, there are a number of things that he or she could look for. Your pixel data will give you all this information and it will show you what features the customer is looking for in their pair of jeans. Once you know the kind of features that attract a customer, you will be able to customize your ads based on that.

Quick Shoppers

Similar to shoppers that take a long time to purchase things, the Facebook pixel will also help you identify shoppers that are very quick in their decision-making. Such customers are very specific with their requirements and they make a decision within a matter of minutes. Based on your pixel data you will be able to customize ads for these customers and help them purchase very quickly. These customers are driven by a call to action and you need to make sure that your ad features that.

Shopping In-Store

There are a number of customers that still prefer walking into a store and purchasing things rather than purchasing online. If you are a business that also has stores across a city or a country, you can use your Facebook ads to promote the stores. You can provide the store location as well as your operating hours along with all the pricing information that will help your audience make a decision.

Chapter 5: Choose The Best Advertising Option For Your Business on Facebook

Facebook advertising comes in a number of forms and you need to make sure that you pick the right advertising method based on your business. Irrespective of what product or service you deal in there is a Facebook option available for you. Here are a few Facebook ad templates that you can use along with some successful examples.

Video Ad

As the name suggests this is an ad that features a video and it will appear in the news feed for your potential users. You need to get as creative as possible with your video because it can help create a very positive impact on the audience. If you are into the food industry then you can show a video of a recipe being made and how it can benefit the users. You can also show gadgets that are featured in your video that can help make life easier in the kitchen. There are various kitchen hacks that you can share with your users in the form of a video and this is something that will definitely create a positive impact. Your audience will know that you care about their comfort rather than trying to sell your own business product.

Take a look at this example of a successful video ad.

http://bit.ly/2UdtRFZ

Photo Ad

Photo ads are generally useful for businesses that deal with products that can be seen. Photo ads are more effective in selling products rather than selling services. For example, if you are in the fashion industry then you can showcase pictures of your products worn by various models and this will help you create a positive outreach. Here is a classic example of a successful photo ad.

http://bit.ly/2TkkZ4f

Reach Ad

A reach ad helps with promoting a particular shop or a product in a local area. For example, if you are having a sale in your local store, you can give information to customers based in that area and also provide details regarding the store. This ad will not show up to people that do not live in that area and this is how your ad can reach the maximum number of people. Reach ads can have a lot of impacts, however, there is a very limited scope because it is only specific to a particular segment. Here is an example of a successful reach advertisement.

http://bit.ly/2NvYiVm

Offer Ad

An offer advertisement helps promote certain offers that your business is bringing up. This will help get more customers interested in your business and you will be able to reach a wider audience irrespective of whether they have been your customers or not in the past. This advertisement will be shown only two people that have shown an interest in a similar product or service as yours. A classic example is if you are a local business that caters to pest control and if a customer has searched for pest control via a search engine, your Facebook ad will show up in the news feed of that particular customer. When you combine this targeting along with an offer ad, there is a very good chance that you will be able to convert a lead into a customer. Here is a very good example of an offer advertisement.

http://bit.ly/2IHNuVE

Event Ad

An event ad is very useful when it comes to promoting events in certain localities or even in certain cities. The event ad will give information regarding the event along with the timings. The event ad also ensures that you reach maximum people and you gain maximum participation for your event. Event ads will only be shown to people that have shown an interest in similar events in the past. Here is a look at a classic event ad.

http://bit.ly/2TjPmb7

Retargeting Ad

Retargeting ad is a generic ad that will help target customers that have shown an interest in your business or are currently contemplating purchasing a product similar to your product. If a customer looks for restaurant listings in his or her area and you are a local restaurant that has newly opened, your ad will appear to this customer and you will be able to get them to eat in your restaurant. In order for your ad to be successful, you need to have certain offers that may interest the customer. You will need to do proper research and prepare your ad based on what customers are looking for. Here is how a retargeting ad should look.

http://bit.ly/2EB3rbR

Targeting Based On The Audience

Facebook is available across multiple platforms and multiple operating systems. This means that every gadget that you have can be used to access Facebook and this makes it easier for you to reach a wider audience. However, you need to make sure that the format is correct irrespective of how the customer is viewing your ad.

Desktop / Laptop

If a customer is accessing Facebook from his or her desktop or laptop, then you will need to showcase your ads in a more traditional format. There are two ways it can showcase your ad to customers. You can choose to display ads on the right side of the screen. This ad will not interfere with the customer's newsfeed and it will be visible to the customer even if he or she keeps scrolling. The other way that you can display your ad on a laptop or a desktop is in the middle of the news feed. While this ad can grab attention, it can also get annoying if the customer keeps seeing your ad again and again. You need to make sure that you are selecting the right criteria for displaying your ads otherwise your ad may be marked as spam if it is being shown to the wrong user.

Mobile User

Almost 90% of all Facebook users access Facebook from their mobile phones. This means that you need to focus on creating the right mobile format for your ads so that the customer does not miss out on the ad and the visual experience is not hampered as well. When a customer is accessing Facebook through their mobile phone the ad will appear in the news feed and you need to make sure that you create the right ad because mobile phone users generally scroll by very quickly. If something does not catch their eye, they will not stop scrolling and you lose your chance of impressing and gaining a customer.

Chapter 6: Ideas And Tips For Ads Using The Persuasion Principles

We've already spoken about the persuasion principles and how they can help create better ads for you. The principles of Dr. Robert Cialdini have been very useful for a number of businesses and his research and training have helped people understand the psychology of influence and how to link it with their marketing efforts. The principles of persuasion will help you get better outreach, drive more customers to your website, increase subscriptions to your newsletters and get more downloads for your app.

Here we will look at the principles of persuasion and how you can use them to create effective Facebook ads.

Reciprocity

Reciprocity is nothing but responding to favor by doing another favor. When someone does not reciprocate, it is considered to be ungrateful. A number of businesses use the principle of reciprocation by offering discounts as well as free samples. The principle of reciprocity can be used in a number of ways to gain more customers, and here is a look at a few examples.

Going with an example of a realtor, you can offer a substantial discount to one of your listings in an area if somebody purchases within X number of days. You can also offer a free consultation or no brokerage if somebody refers to a customer to you within the next month. If you are running a restaurant, then you can offer discounts to your regular customers in order for them to come back to you in the future. You can even offer a membership program where customers would get a fixed discount each time they visit your restaurant.

Consistency and Commitment

This principle is all about retargeting your audience. There are two advantages of retargeting. One is you will always be the number one choice for a customer because you want them to come back to you. Customers like it when a business makes them feel important and want them to return as customers. The second advantage is customers start trusting you because they have availed of your services in the past. The principle of commitment and consistency will hold true when you keep delivering the best products to your customers over and over again. This shows the ability to commit and deliver quality products and the consistency to deliver this product over a period of time.

Here we again look at an example of a realtor. If you are in the business of real estate and you have various open houses coming up, you should contact customers that have purchased from you in the past. No one said that you cannot purchase more than one house at a time. Your customers will also feel honored that you consider retargeting them when it comes to a new house being sold. A restaurant can also retarget its customers by offering discounts from time to time or reminding customers of important dates coming up in their life. Wishing customers happy birthday on their birthday or offering discounts in the birthday month are a few of the things that will hold true to this principle.

Social Proof

The principle of social proof is based on your online reviews as well as endorsements by influencers or celebrities. When there is collective approval for your product your customers will not hesitate choosing you over a competitor. In the case of a realtor, if you have successfully sold in the past and your customers leave positive reviews online there is no reason new buyers would not approach you. Online reviews are a great way to ensure that you keep getting new customers and it is the greatest form of publicity. When it comes to picking a restaurant most customers would read reviews online before they choose any particular restaurant. If you are a local business and there is a lot of competition you can request the local influencer to leave a positive review online that will help other customers come to your restaurant.

The Principle of Liking

The principle of liking is very similar to social proof. If customers see a particular product or service being promoted by a celebrity that they like, there is a very good chance that they will pick that product over other products. As a realtor, you may want to get somebody to promote your page. This person could be an influencer or it could also be a celebrity that a lot of people like. The same can be done for a restaurant. Promoting your restaurant page online through an influencer or a celebrity is something that works in your favor and many people will queue up to make reservations because they believe in your product.

Authority

The principle of authority is also based on the principle of liking. People will usually opt for a product that is promoted by an authority that they believe in. If you are promoting a particular product or service you can have a social figure or an authority promoting your business. In the example of a real estate business, you can get local celebrities to give a seminar on the changing face of real estate and why it is good to invest today. You could even hire real estate authority figures that people trust. When it comes to a restaurant, people are very particular about the kind of food that they eat. With the help of an authority figure in the culinary world, you will be able to get more people to pick your restaurant over a competitor.

Scarcity

Scarcity is a very common persuasion principle that is used by businesses all over the world. Scarcity usually creates urgency and this helps in selling products and services quicker. In the example of a realtor, you need to offer a limited time discount as well as free open houses that will attract more buyers towards your business. In a restaurant business, it is very easy to implement the principle of scarcity. All you need to do is offer a free meal or a buy-one-get-one-free offer depending on what festivities are coming up or if there is any occasion that is approaching. Giving a limited time offer will make sure that your restaurant will do more business than any other restaurant in your area.

Now that you understood the principles of persuasion in detail and you have seen the kind of ads that can be created based on each of the principles, you can go ahead and create an ad based on each of the principles. Make sure that your ad takes into account what the concept of each principle is and how it can convince the user to pick your product or service over anyone else. You need to be subtle while applying the principle because customers usually do not prefer an ad that is too pushy or direct to the point.

Chapter 7: When It All Comes Together: The Plan

Now that you understood what Facebook marketing is all about you will need to come up with ways to bring all the learnings together and implement it properly. One of the first things that you need to do is create a content calendar. A content calendar helps you to create engaging content and create brand awareness. This calendar will help you improve customer engagement and will also help with your SEO efforts. A calendar will help you plan your content across various platforms. You can either create this content calendar for a month or the next couple of weeks. It does not have to be an extravagant calendar that is very detailed. It could be a simple spreadsheet that will help you note down the dates along with the content that needs to be published. This will not only help you maintain consistency with your content, but it will also help you stay organized. Here are the benefits of maintaining a content calendar.

Implement an organized Content Strategy

A content calendar will help you stay organized across platforms for the duration that you created the calendar.

When it comes to content on Facebook you need to make sure that it is consistent and regular. When you do not have a content calendar in place, you will usually panic and end up creating posts just for the heck of it. This is bound to create no impact and you will end up losing a lot of your followers that you already have. When your audience sees that you are putting no efforts towards your posts, they will lose interest in your business as well, and this will not be great for your development. When you know that you have to post content later on in the day, you will keep the content ready well in advance. A content calendar will help you stay organized by pushing you towards publishing content and creating quality content for important dates that could be coming up. For example, creating content for Valentine's Day or remembrance day or the fourth of July.

Save On Time

With the content calendar in place, you will be able to save on a lot of time because most of your content would be organized and ready to publish. When you are not spending too much time stressing about your Facebook marketing, you will be able to focus on other important aspects of your business and this will help your business grow along with creating brand awareness through Facebook. A content calendar will also help you pre-schedule posts so that you can ensure your Facebook marketing is happening even if you do not physically log in to Facebook and check the same.

Create Content Well In Advance

When you do not have a content calendar, you will suddenly realize that you need to post regarding a certain event today. Imagine you are on your way to the airport for a business trip and on the way you realize that today is memorial day. If you do not post on Memorial Day there is a very good chance that people will get offended because your business did not care about an important holiday. You will then be forced to create content while you are on the go and this is something that is not recommended. When content is created on the go, it looks rushed and it will not be very creative, as well. A content calendar will help you create your content at least a couple of days in advance. This will ensure that the content that you publish is timely and top quality.

You Can Create A Strategy

When you run a Facebook marketing campaign you will need a strategy in place. Publishing random posts on your Facebook page will not really get you anywhere because the audience will not see the connection between your posts. Most big brands will have a strategy as far as their posts are concerned and you will see that most of the posts are consistent towards a certain strategy. With the help of the content calendar, you will be able to create a strategy and implement it properly.

When you are marketing on Facebook there are a number of ways to get carried away and you will end up wasting a lot of time as well as money. There are certain things that you should not do when you are focusing on Facebook marketing. Here are a few tips that will help you save time and money.

Stop Building Facebook Apps

There are a number of ideas that are floating out there and they tend to suggest that this could be the next big Facebook app. You will end up spending a lot of time and effort in building the app because most of the concepts are never successful. The Facebook experts that suggest building these apps also claim that the app will bring in a lot of new customers as well as new fans. That is far from the truth. The best thing to do is to pick up an app that has already been built by a developer. This will help you save on a lot of time and money and you will also be able to target the right audience with the money that you saved.

Picking the Wrong Prize For Your Contest

Facebook comes down very firmly on clickbaits and it often bans ads that hide content from users until they share certain posts on Facebook. If you want to hold a contest you should ask a simple question and give away a price that is relevant to your business. If you are in the restaurant business you could give away a gift voucher that will gift a dinner for two or you could even offer lifetime membership to the customer to a gym that you may be running in the local area.

Post Educational Content

If you want people to start liking your post and you want organic followers on Facebook then you need to start posting content that is relevant to the audience and will add value. You need to make sure that you are posting information that will be useful and not just promoting your business. You should also try to personalize your posts and make sure that you connect with your audience in the right manner.

Stop Wasting Time on Facebook

A number of business owners end up wasting days on end trying to figure out what kind of ads to post and at what time to post them. As a business owner, you need to invest in post managers that will help you understand what kind of posts would be relevant to your business and when you should post them. These post managers will help you understand the right kind of audience and they will also help you post the right kind of content.

Don't Purchase Fans

Purchasing fans to increase your followers on Facebook is like getting mannequins to come and stand at your live event. These fans are not relevant and will never add value to Facebook. Try to attract organic fans by posting interesting information regularly.

Get More Out Of Your Ad Results

Not every business has unlimited resources as well as a limited budget that will help towards Facebook marketing. While every business wants to succeed, you need to make sure that you use your resources properly so that you make the most of your Facebook advertisements. In order to use Facebook advertisements effectively here are a few tips that you need to keep in mind. These steps will ensure that you spend minimum time on Facebook and get the maximum benefit out of it.

Choose Your Tools Wisely

Facebook has a number of inbuilt tools that will help you with your ad management but you need to make sure that you are selecting the right tools. There are many changes that Facebook makes on a daily basis. Using the right tool will help you promote your product in a better manner and save on a lot of money. For example, if you are selling only one product, there is no point in using the Facebook carousel ad. This format is used to display different products from a single brand. When you are looking to sell one product then you should select the single image ad.

Choose Quality Over Quantity

Login into Facebook 10 times a day and posting 10 irrelevant posts is not going to make much of a difference if the posts do not have a positive impact. Rather than spending the entire day on Facebook and publishing a lot of posts, you need to select two or three posts that will make an impact and use the rest of your time improving your business.

Targeting The Right Audience

You need to use Facebook targeting tools to your advantage. Rather than promoting your ad to millions of users across Facebook and getting no results, you need to target the right audience and get maximum outreach. You need to also target the right geographic areas so that your business can grow within the budget constraints that you have.

Chapter 8: Email and Email marketing

Targeting your customers through email marketing is a very important aspect that you need to focus on. While Facebook marketing is important, you should use it to your advantage and collect as many email leads as possible. These emails will help you connect with your leads through your email marketing efforts and it will ensure that you continue connecting with them even after they have converted to a customer. Facebook keeps changing on a daily basis and there are various algorithms that could be introduced that may block access to your Facebook page. In such a scenario it will be very difficult for you to build a customer base overnight if you have no information about who your followers were and what their contact information was. This is where your email list will come very handy. You need to keep collecting emails on a daily basis to ensure that you promote your business to potential leads in the right manner.

Facebook Marketing Versus Email Marketing

Business owners usually offer Facebook marketing over email marketing because they believe that most of their audience is on Facebook. They are not wrong because Facebook marketing is definitely trending these days and going with the trend generally works in your favor. The one thing that you should remember is you should never stop your email marketing campaigns because it has its own benefits. There are a number of differences between email marketing and Facebook marketing and this section will let you know what the differences are and what benefits you gain from each of these marketing campaigns.

The Difference

The big difference between Facebook followers versus email subscribers is your email subscriber list is usually your current customer base and your Facebook followers are potential leads. You will have complete control over your email subscription list whereas you do not control your Facebook followers. Most of your current customers will always opt-in for your email marketing campaigns because they have used your services in the past and they know that you can be trusted. Facebook followers are not necessarily your current customers and they may never be. You will need to put in more effort towards converting your Facebook followers into customers while that is not the case with your email subscribers.

If you compare the people that use email on a daily basis versus Facebook on a daily basis, you will realize that the numbers almost double up. Almost 90% of people will use their email on a daily basis because that is a way of communicating with other businesses as well as their family members and friends. Facebook is a casual activity and almost 60% of users use it on a daily basis. Facebook is used primarily to check in with family members and friends and see what is happening around the world. If you have to communicate with someone professionally then you will come to your email rather than Facebook. The click-through rate for emails is higher than the click-through rate for Facebook marketing.

The Reach

The one question you need to ask as a business owner is how many people check their mailbox before they check Facebook on a daily basis? Once you get the answer to this question you will know which of the marketing campaigns are more effective. Most of your serious customers will always check their mailbox before they check Facebook because they expect important emails from different people in their lives. This could be emails from other businesses or even from their loved ones, and in some cases from their boss. Most people would turn to Facebook only when they have nothing much to do during the day.

Getting Traffic to Your Facebook

Ads

The main purpose of Facebook marketing should be to get more people to your website. When people start clicking on your website or visiting your blog you can ask them to subscribe to your notifications and this will help you get the email IDs regularly. with is where Facebook marketing can help you tremendously. When you are selecting the purpose of your marketing campaign, you should make sure that you specify promoting a website and enter the URL of your website. You can use a single image ad for this promotion and get maximum people to your website through your Facebook marketing campaigns. The more people that come to your website, the more subscriptions you get and the more email IDs you collect.

Create a Landing Page within Your Facebook Ad

Apart from having a call to action, you also need to have a landing page on your Facebook ad. This landing page will usually divert all traffic to your website and it will help you generate more leads. All the leads that you get through the landing page would be potential customers because these are people that are interested in your product and that is the reason they clicked on the link. The landing page needs to be strong and should capture the attention of the audience. There are various landing page builders that you can opt-in for and these builders will help you create a very professional-looking and effective landing page.

Create the Right Campaign For Your Email Ids

When you have collated your email IDs, you need to have a strategy in place that will help nurture the leads. It is important to make people feel welcome and not spam them with emails 4 to 5 times a day. You need to send a welcome email as soon as somebody subscribes to your mailing list and you need to follow up on your leads effectively. With the help of a welcome email, you will be able to connect personally with subscribers. You can even send out birthday wishes or anniversary wishes based on the information that you have regarding the leads.

Ways to Collect Leads From Your Facebook Campaign

There are a few effective tools that you can use to your advantage and collect email IDs through your Facebook marketing campaign. The steps are very useful and it will help you get maximum fans to subscribe to your email list. Here are the best ways to collect email IDs from your Facebook fans.

Create A Signup Form

This is a very effective method of collecting emails and a number of businesses use this basic method of getting people to subscribe to their mailing list. There are a number of email service providers that will help create a signup form and you can integrate this with your Facebook tab. You can also try and promote your subscriber list on your Facebook page.

Offering Incentives

Another way of getting email IDs is by offering something in return. This can be seen with the example of the restaurant. If you want to start running email marketing campaigns for your restaurant then you will need people to subscribe to your mailing list. As a restaurant owner, you need to make sure that you are offering something in return so that people give you their email IDs. The best way to do this is by offering people a flat discount when they arrive at your restaurant. All you need to do is offer the customers a survey form that they can fill out and receive a 5% discount in return.

Organize A Contest

Most fans get very excited with the prospect of winning something out of a contest. People would enter any survey form just so they can receive rewards. If we take the example of the realtor, you can offer exclusive open houses to people that have subscribed to your email list. Most people love exclusivity and they will do just about anything to get their hands on a top property before anyone else.

The habit of browsing through Facebook is usually done while traveling or when you are sitting for lunch or maybe when you take a quick 5-minute break. The seriousness associated with email marketing is a lot more compared to Facebook marketing. Most of the ads that you will see on Facebook prove to be clickbaits and this is what diminishes the trust factor for Facebook marketing. While the same can be said about emails, the percentage of clickbaits is a lot lower and most email clients have a built-in spam filter that will keep unwanted emails away.

Chapter 9: Improve, Test, Grow, and Monetize

Your content is extremely important when it comes to attracting customers on Facebook. While there are a number of content tips that we have spoken about, you should always focus on creating content that will keep your audience engaged. Here are a few tips that you need to keep in mind when generating content for Facebook marketing.

Mix Up Your Content

Irrespective of what kind of business you are into, you need to make sure that you make new posts and publish content in different formats. Facebook allows you to create ads in different formats and you should use that to your advantage. You can choose to publish a blog post every week that will help customers understand what your business is up to and what has happened in the past. You can even get people to subscribe to your blog post by inserting a call to action at the end. Another way of sharing content is with the help of photos. Rather than downloading images from search engines you need to take live snapshots of your workers as well as customers and post them on your Facebook page. You should even post pictures from events that you have hosted or any of the marketing strategies that you have tried. You should also keep publishing press releases every now and then. Press releases are a professional way of communicating with your customers and informing them about any updates that are coming up. This is also a great way of informing people of any new store openings or a new sale that may be coming up by the end of the month.

Encourage Posts from Your Fans

As the name suggests, you run a fan page and not a business page. This means you will need to give fans the opportunity to voice their opinion. You should not be scared of negative comments because that is going to happen irrespective of whether your fans can post on your page or not. Encourage fans to post success stories on your wall and tell the world how Facebook has made a difference in their life. The success stories will encourage other potential leads to become customers because they know that this content has not been created by the business but it has been created by a live customer. This is like a Facebook review but in the form of a post on a wall.

Use Contest in Moderation

While it is advisable to announce contests every now and then, you should not overdo the contests because it takes away the excitement. Most of the fans will end up following your business page just because you are running contests regularly and not because they are interested in your product.

Create Interesting Content

While you are a professional business and you want to have serious information posted on your fan page, there is no point being serious all the time. You need to inject a bit of humor in your posts because this will help your fan page to stand out and get more followers.

Define your USP

Every business needs to have a unique selling point that will help them stand out from the crowd. You need to make sure that your USP is very different and you offer something that no one else does. This does not necessarily have to be a product, it can even be a service that you are offering. There are a number of brands that promote their customer service rather than promoting their product. This is because there are millions of products out there but very few brands that offer brilliant customer service. You need to come up with a USP based on what your customers think your strong point is and the feedback that you received. Your USP also depends on your target audience and what you are offering them. For example, your audience could be looking for a product that helps them save on time or a product that is trustworthy. If your brand is offering these value additions to the customer, then you will be able to claim that as your USP.

Your USP can change depending on the kind of business you are in and the target customers that you have. You need to deliver on what you promise and based on that you can claim your selling point. When you know what your USP is, all your communication should focus on this USP and your company vision should also be based around it. Always communicate your USP clearly and make sure that you are providing it in every offering as well. Don't try changing a USP too often because it will take away the identity of the business. Here are a few things you need to keep in mind when you are creating a USP:

- make sure you know who your target audience is.
- try to note down all the ways that your product or service could help people. This will help become a very strong selling point for your business.
- compare your selling point with your competitor and see what they are proposing. Make sure that your proposition is unique and it will help you capture a majority share in the market.
- conduct surveys with your potential customers as well as your current customers and see what they feel your USP is.
- monitor the current trends and see how your customers

are being affected and whether you will be able to provide a solution.

Targeting Current Customers

Most businesses make the mistake of ignoring their current customers and focusing on new leads. This is because business owners feel that if a customer has purchased once from their business, they will always rely on their business in the future as well. The fact remains that every business still needs to compete with other businesses for their current customers as well. Brand loyalty is built over a number of years and not just over a couple of purchases. The example of a restaurant or a soft drink is more relevant. If a customer has been going to a restaurant to eat for the past decade along with his family members it would be very difficult for any other restaurant to convince him otherwise. However, if someone had a single meal at a pizza joint, it doesn't mean that the customer will be loyal to the pizza joint. As a business owner, you need to make sure that you are looking to improve your brand in order to retain your current customers. While email marketing is very effective in retargeting customers, you also need to make the most of Facebook marketing and get more customers to do repeat business with you.

When you are running a business you need to make sure that you use Facebook marketing to your advantage and see what the current customers feel about your products or services.

You need to make sure that you live up to the expectations of your customers because their brand loyalty and their views are going to be vital in you acquiring new customers. You need to test and see what your customers like and what they are not happy with. If you feel that your product could solve another problem that your customers are facing, you need to communicate with the customer and make them aware of the solution that you are offering.

It is important that your business keeps evolving as time goes by. Let us take the example of a real estate business. If you have sold properties to various customers in the past decade, you need to look at those customers once again and see if they want to move into a bigger apartment or if their current apartment is giving them some problems. The one area where most realtors fail is not following up with their current customers because they feel that they cannot get any more business out of them. However, that is far from the truth. If you have sold the wrong house to a customer you need to make up for that mistake because word of mouth publicity can put you down in no time. There is no shortage of realtors in the market today and if your potential buyers learn about the way you do business, they will avoid you. You should always look for the benefit of your current customers before you move to generate new leads. This is where Facebook marketing can help you. You can target your current customers by checking how they feel about the last purchase that they made. Try conducting a survey to see if any of your current customers are unhappy and communicate with them if you feel that there is something that you can do better for them.

The Ladder of Engagement

The ladder of engagement has been created to improve engagement between a business and its potential customers. Most business owners are not able to relate to their customers because they are not sure what it takes to encourage more engagement from the customer. This is where a ladder of engagement helps. This ladder encourages you to take one step at a time and this will gradually help build a strong relationship with your customer base.

Start Easy

When you build your Facebook page you need to start slowly and ask your audience to do small tasks for you. These tasks could involve sharing your fan page with their family members, and friends, clicking on your website link or subscribing to your email list. None of these tasks require too much time investment from the customer's end and they will be more than happy to do it. Once your customers have completed these tasks they will be ready to perform even bigger tasks for your business.

Collect Key Data

As the engagement level between the customer and the business increases, the collection of data should also increase. You need to collect information such as email ID, name of the customer, location, along with interests. This will help you customize your communication with the customer in the future and it will help build on the initial engagement.

Don't Demand Too Much

Let us again take the example of the restaurant. If you want more people to come and become a customer at your restaurant you should not directly ask for it. Instead, you need to put it in the form of suggestions made by your current customers. You are allowed to rope in big-name celebrities or local influencers that will help create a positive impact.

Expand the Ladder of Engagement

Once you have reached a level where you are communicating effectively with your customers, you need to make sure that you expand the ladder further. This can be done in the form of asking people to help your business grow in your local area. If you are struggling, you can go ahead and ask local investors to come in and take over a percentage of your business in return for an investment. Since the level of engagement is so high, many people will come forward and it will help your business survive even in an aggressive market.

Tell Stories as Part of Your Facebook Campaign

Storytelling is extremely important and you will be able to connect to the audience in a better manner. A number of brands tell stories to reach a high level of connection with their customers and you need to do the same as well. There are a number of advantages that storytelling has to offer and it will help with your marketing efforts tremendously. If you target your Facebook campaigns based on the emotional response of the customer, you will end up reaching a wider audience. People usually connect with a story a lot more than a marketing campaign. There are various kinds of stories that can help your business get its point across. Here is how you can tell the stories effectively.

Focus On the Issues At Hand

As a business owner, you always need to look at the trends that are happening and how they are affecting your customers. There are a number of issues that need to be taken care of and this can be done through your Facebook marketing campaign. If you feel that racism is on the rise, then you can create a video celebrating different ethnicities and showing that unity is what prevails. You need to come up with a story that will touch the heart of your audience and they will be compelled to share the story forward. There are a number of big brands that are using storytelling to their advantage and it is working.

Connect With the Audience

Try and relate to the problems that your customers are facing and put forward your product as a solution to the problems. You will see the biggest cosmetic brands touching on the most sensitive issues that are happening around the world today and telling a story around that. In most cultures color is usually a problem and most big guns will point out that this is wrong. Acceptability in society is something that everyone is entitled to and when you tell a story around such a sensitive issue people that are affected by this will relate to your brand.

Try and Relate With the Problems That the Customer Is Facing

There are different segments of people that face different kinds of problems on a daily basis. Some parents facing an issue with their children not respecting them while others face a problem with their children not even visiting them when they are old. Some children face neglect in life while others are harassed in school and college. If you can create awareness as a business owner around these issues, you will be able to get the right message across and create an impact in society. Most people are not even aware of what's happening around them and releasing a short video on the realities of society can be an eye-opener for many people.

Storytelling is very powerful and you need to make sure that you use it in the right manner. Promoting the wrong stories or giving false information is not going to hold you in good stead. Apart from helping you grow your business, the story should also make a difference in society and that is what you should be aiming for.

How To Stop People From Scrolling Past Your Post?

Facebook marketing is extremely important and you need to create the right kind of posts in order to get people's attention. Spending hundreds and thousands of dollars on Facebook advertising will not really be helpful if your ad campaigns are not powerful enough. You should never be satisfied with the number of followers that you have and look to acquire some new followers on a daily basis. The only way this can be done is when your posts are reaching more people. There are various reasons why a post may not be going viral and you need to figure out what can be done in order to attract more attention. Here are a few tips that you can keep in mind in order to create engaging posts on Facebook.

Understand the Platform

Facebook business pages are not very complicated and you need to understand how to use it in order to come across as a professional outfit. Sharing random images or putting up a random text on your fan page will get you nowhere. You need to make sure that you understand how the advertisements work and how to create content that will be engaging.

Understanding Your Audience

You should always be aware of what your audience needs when you are posting content online. If your ideal age group is above the age of 40 then there is no point posting information regarding the latest trends in hairstyles. You need to make sure that you're posting information that will be useful to your audience and not something that may offend them.

Use Pictures Relevant To Your Business

Downloading images from the internet and posting them on your business page is not going to benefit anybody. You need to start posting images that are relevant to your business and unique. If ten businesses use the same image, they will not have an identity of their own and their fans will stop relating to them. Also if you use an image of another business post then fans may scroll past the post thinking that the post is from that same business and not yours. You need to create an identity for yourself and make sure that you are posting images that are only unique to you.

Ask Question through Your Post

As a business owner, you need to realize what will make people stop and look at your post. When people are presented with a question or a riddle they will stop and think about it for a couple of seconds before they scroll past. Those few seconds are all you need to create an impact and make people click on your post. You need to make sure that you are catching the imagination of your audience in a matter of seconds. Posting generic content without an interesting headline is not going to be beneficial and 99% of your audience will scroll past your post.

Create Engaging Video Content

Publishing posts and blogs on your Facebook page can be relatively easy, however, creating and posting videos is not that straightforward. You need to keep a lot of tips in mind in order to create a video that will catch the attention of your audience.

Create a Sharp Video

Most videos start off with a boring introduction and this is where the audience loses interest. Make a video that gets straight to the point and does not waste the time of the user. The best way to do this is by eliminating unnecessary content from the video and choosing a thumbnail image that will make the user click on the video.

Use Captions Effectively

Not many people play videos with the sound enabled on it. This could be because they are at work or they would be traveling and they do not want to disturb others around them. When creating a video you should make sure that you caption it properly so that people would be able to understand the video even if the sound is off. This will keep the user engaged because without proper captions or sound, your video may seem confusing and you will lose the user.

Choose the Right Title

The title plays a huge part in capturing the imagination of the audience. You need to make sure that you are choosing your title wisely and you need to use appropriate keywords that will help increase the visibility of the video as well.

Create a Short Description

Facebook allows you to post a short description of your video. This description will help your audience understand what is in the video and why they should click on it. This is extremely important because the thumbnail may not interest them but the content of the video may be interesting.

Always Include a Call to Action

No Facebook ad is complete if you do not add a call to action in it. This holds true for a video as well. You need to make sure that you are adding a call to action, either during the video or at the end of it. This will help the audience engage with you and you will be able to make full use of the effectiveness of the video with the help of the call to action.

Understanding Content Marketing

Content marketing is extremely crucial in today's date and you need to focus on having the right strategy in order to be successful. A number of business owners go to great lengths in getting the right content for their campaigns. Apart from having engaging content, you also need to look at strategies to get more content from various sources. You need to look at effective ways of content marketing and how it can be useful to your business. You could market your content through various methods on Facebook. However, you should know what the strong points for your business are and whether it will be useful to you or not. Here is a look at the various content types that are available on Facebook and how it can prove to be beneficial to your business.

Video Streaming

The concept of video streaming has caught on in the past year or so and it is one of the biggest trends on Facebook right now. A number of celebrities use live video streaming to connect with their audience and a number of businesses also use this method to promote or launch new products. The problem with a live video feed is that almost every business is doing the same thing and the audience will eventually get bored of it. While it is an effective way of promoting your business, you need to make sure that you are not creating a live video for every ad that you post on Facebook.

Engage With Your Audience

No matter what business you are in, you need to make sure that you are soliciting some kind of response from your audience through your Facebook marketing campaign. Most businesses try and introduce a poll that will help the audience get involved with your business. Some businesses also publish maps or quizzes in order to capture the attention of the audience.

Online Webinars or Courses

The internet has made the world smaller and a number of businesses are offering their services online as opposed to offering it physically. Education is one such field that is constantly evolving. If you are in the field of education, you no longer need to conduct physical classes around the city. You can offer online courses and cover twice as many students as you did when you conducted classes in local areas. The reason students prefer online courses is that it offers the flexibility of timings and it also allows students to takes up more than one course at a time.

Influencer marketing

Influencer marketing is another trend that is growing by the day and a number of large businesses as well as small businesses are turning to influencers in order to increase their fanbase. Depending on the budget for your business, you can choose a local influencer or a national influencer. The best part about having an influencer is they will help create an impact instantly and their fanbase will automatically convert into a fanbase for your business.

Look For Inspiration

There are a number of places where you can find inspiration for your Facebook posts. Your audience wants to see something new on a daily basis and the only way you will be able to give them something new is by being inspired. Looking at unorthodox places for inspiration can prove to be beneficial for you.

Online Galleries

There are a number of online galleries that will give you ideas for your visual ads. These galleries will also help you find inspiration for your text posts as well as headlines. If you are in the publishing business then you can find inspiration for your book covers as well as poster designs.

Product Descriptions

Most of the inspiration for your post comes from your previous work. If you are stuck with a particular post on Facebook, you can go back and see the work that you've done. There always comes a time when a business is very proud of the way it handles itself in the marketing world. You should always look back on these moments and see the product descriptions that you had created at that time. These product descriptions will provide you with amazing ideas and it will help you create engaging content once again.

Go for A Walk

This may sound cliché, but it is very effective. Going out for a walk and clearing your head is an excellent way to get new ideas for your latest content. When you have no distractions around you, your mind will be a lot sharper and you will be able to get ideas almost instantly. If you are looking to get inspiration, you can even take a walk by the beach or a calm lake.

Check Out Customer Surveys

Customer surveys are a great way of getting more information and new ideas. If you have already conducted a survey in the past then it's a great time to take it out and see what your customers think about your product. If you have never conducted a survey then there is no harm doing one right now.

You need to find out a few things from your survey. You need to get feedback regarding the products and services that you are offering, you need to understand what people's expectations are from your brand and you need to understand where you are going wrong. Once you get the answer to these questions you will be able to get ideas and promote your business in a more effective manner.

Fashion Magazines

Believe it or not, fashion magazines have a lot of well-written content that can provide inspiration for your next Facebook post. Most fashion magazines approach the top writers for their content because it is a very competitive field. If the top magazines do not deliver content that is relevant or up to the mark, they will lose their readership in no time.

Quotes

Quotes are highly motivational and they can help you get some interesting ideas on what you can post to Facebook. Try looking for relevant posts that describe the kind of work you do or your business in any way and use them to your advantage. Whenever you quote someone remember to give them credit by mentioning the name in the post. You can do something creative with a quote by creating an image and using some sort of picture in the background, or even a simple text that can blend in with a relevant link or product your business offers.

Trending News

Keeping an eye on the news and checking out what's trending is definitely a great way to design your posts. Seasonal posts and posts around the time of a festival definitely need to be customized and more in sync with the flavor of the season. Incorporate posts in a manner that reflects a current trend because that's would people look out for. During Christmas, try having the entire holiday festive season theme posts because these do really well around that time.

See What Your Competition Is Up To

One of the best ways to get inspiration is by looking around you. This does not only include looking at the things that you love but you can also look at your competition. Sometimes your direct competitors may have better ideas and there is no harm in getting inspiration from their posts. If you look at the biggest advertising wars for the past decade, you will see that competitors have been swiping ideas from each other and taking a dig at them in the process. While you do not need to go ahead and make things ugly, ensuring that you look to them for inspiration is a very sensible thing to do. There is no harm in admitting that your competition is better than you in terms of ideas and the only way you can get better is by getting inspired.

Conclusion

Facebook marketing is perfect for small businesses and there are a number of entities that are still not sure of how it can work to their benefit. With the help of this guide, you can now understand how a business owner can take his business forward without having to spend too much money on marketing efforts. The reason Facebook marketing is so effective is that it has a wide outreach and there are a number of tools that are available for the business to use. A number of business owners have turned to social media marketing in the last decade and this trend will keep continuing because of the marketing tools that social media channels provide. Without the right social media interaction, business owners would not be able to make an impact in the market.

If you look at the most successful businesses, you will realize that Facebook marketing has been an integral part of their journey. While some businesses move forward and choose other channels of marketing, their initial base would have been created with the help of Facebook marketing and this is something that cannot be replicated. Since Facebook provides a large variety of posts, you will be able to make the right decision and choose the right tools to help your business move forward. Facebook is also very helpful when it comes to interacting with your current client base as well as your new potential customers.

You can combine Facebook marketing along with the principles of persuasion and have the perfect marketing strategy to help your business grow. Facebook is a continuous marketing effort and it never stops showcasing your business to your intended targets. All you need to do is make sure that you engage your audience with the right kind of content and tell stories that will help you connect with society. Establishing a brand with the help of Facebook marketing is not that easy. You just need to look at a few successful examples out there and try and replicate their marketing strategies to help your business grow. Apart from providing you with effective solutions, Facebook will also contribute towards making your business bigger than it currently is. If you follow the steps correctly you will realize that Facebook marketing is all about the right content and the right strategy.

If you are looking to run a successful business you need to make sure that your time management, as well as money-management skills, are up to the mark. There is no such thing as a perfect solution and you need to work towards building the right brand for your business. You need to work towards defining a business strategy and this book will help you achieve this.

Instagram promotions are limited to images and videos, hence you can't experiment too much. There's a limited audience on Instagram and if you're looking for a crowd that is serious and professional, then Instagram won't work as well. Instagram may not be as effective as you want it to be and this is the reason a number of businesses prefer choosing Facebook over other social media channels. With Facebook, you will even be able to experiment with your target audience and find out their likes and dislikes. Instagram would not give you much of an option as far as understanding your buyer profile is concerned. Another advantage of Facebook over Instagram is you will no longer have to spend time finding the right audience because Facebook tools do that for you. You will no longer have to worry about how you will find potential buyers for your business. Using the Facebook tools correctly will ensure you build your brand name in no time.

It's important to focus on a method that works and helps you generate potential customers and leads for your business. Converting these leads into actual customers is the next phase of marketing which involves the use of an effective sales funnel. Sign up for my newsletter and I'll let you in on an extra chapter about how you can use the sales funnel to step up your efforts on social media and get more customers to your business. It's time to begin your journey from a small business to an established brand with the key persuasion principles and the right knowledge of marketing & online sales.

Bibliography

11 Principles That Need to Power Your Facebook Strategy. (2019). Retrieved from https://www.postplanner.com/blog/principles-to-power-your-Facebook-strategy

8 Strategies for Achieving SMART Goals. (2019). Project Smart. Retrieved 13 March 2019, from https://www.projectsmart.co.uk/8-strategies-for-achieving-smart-goals.php

Stec, C. (2019). How to Create Facebook Ads: A Step-by-Step Guide to Advertising on Facebook. Blog.hubspot.com. Retrieved 13 March 2019, from https://blog.hubspot.com/marketing/Facebook-paid-ad-checklist

Easy to Follow 7 Step Facebook Marketing Strategy That Works. (2018). Digital Marketing Blog. Retrieved 13 March 2019, from https://www.lyfemarketing.com/blog/Facebook-marketing-strategy/

Baker, J. (2018). 11 Best Social Media Scripts and Plugins to Streamline Your Workflow. Code Envato Tuts+. Retrieved 13 March 2019, from https://code.tutsplus.com/articles/best-social-media-scripts-and-plugins-to-streamline-your-workflow--cms-31941

Bullas, J. (2017). 21 Awesome Facebook Facts and Statistics You Must Check Out. Jeffbullas's Blog. Retrieved 13 March

2019, from https://www.jeffbullas.com/21-awesome-Facebook-facts-and-statistics-you-need-to-check-out/

What Do People Look for in Social Media? | Bearly Marketing. (2015). Bearly Marketing. Retrieved 13 March 2019, from https://bearlymarketing.com/what-do-people-look-for-in-social-media/

Trends, S., Daily, 5., & Guta, M. (2018). 52% of Small Businesses Post on Social Media Daily - Small Business Trends. Small Business Trends. Retrieved 13 March 2019, from https://smallbiztrends.com/2018/03/how-small-businesses-use-social-media-in-2018.html

StyleShare. (2019). Facebook Business. Retrieved 13 March 2019, from https://www.facebook.com/business/success/styleshare

Hawooo & Smartly.io. (2019). Facebook Business. Retrieved 13 March 2019, from https://www.facebook.com/business/success/hawoo-smartly-io#

Kakao Games & Wisebirds. (2019). Facebook Business. Retrieved 13 March 2019, from https://www.facebook.com/business/success/kakao-games-wisebirds#

PlayKids. (2019). Facebook Business. Retrieved 13 March 2019, from https://www.facebook.com/business/success/playkids#

15 ways to enhance your Facebook influence . (2011).

Socialbrite. Retrieved 13 March 2019, from http://www.socialbrite.org/2011/02/08/15-ways-to-enhance-your-Facebook-influence/

13 Quick Tips to Save Time on Facebook Marketing. (2019). Postplanner.com. Retrieved 13 March 2019, from https://www.postplanner.com/blog/13-tips-to-save-time-on-Facebook-marketing/

Us, A., Robert Cialdini, P., Biography, D., Publications, D., Vitae, C., & Services, F. et al. (2019). The 6 Principles of Persuasion by Dr. Robert Cialdini [Official Site]. INFLUENCE AT WORK. Retrieved 13 March 2019, from https://www.influenceatwork.com/principles-of-persuasion/

Influence — The Psychology of Persuasion — A Book Summary. (2018). Medium. Retrieved 13 March 2019, from https://medium.com/power-books/influence-the-psychology-of-persuasion-a-book-summary-7ae0ebf8950f

→, V. (2012). Summary of Influence: The Psychology of Persuasion by Robert B Cialdini. Ignition Blog. Retrieved 13 March 2019, from https://slooowdown.wordpress.com/2012/09/02/summary-of-influence-the-psychology-of-persuasion-by-robert-b-cialdini/

Book Summary: "Influence: The Psychology of Persuasion" by Robert B. Cialdini. (2014). ashishb.net. Retrieved 13 March 2019, from https://ashishb.net/book-summary/book-summary-influence-the-psychology-of-persuasion-by-robert-b-cialdini/

works, H., Agencies, F., e-Commerce, F., Businesses, F., Advertiser, F., Features, A., & Examples, F. (2016). Using Facebook Ads to Find Your Perfect Customer. AdEspresso. Retrieved 13 March 2019, from https://adespresso.com/blog/using-Facebook-ads-to-find-your-perfect-customer/

The Beginner's Guide to Creating Marketing Personas | Buffer. (2015). Buffer Marketing Library. Retrieved 13 March 2019, from https://buffer.com/library/marketing-personas-beginners-guide

How to Build a Buyer Persona (Includes Free Template). (2018). Hootsuite Social Media Management. Retrieved 13 March 2019, from https://blog.hootsuite.com/buyer-persona/

Kolowich, L. (2019). 20 Questions to Ask When Creating Buyer Personas [Free Template]. Blog.hubspot.com. Retrieved 13 March 2019, from https://blog.hubspot.com/marketing/buyer-persona-questions

7 Killer Tips for More Effective Real Estate Facebook Ads. (2019). Wordstream.com. Retrieved 13 March 2019, from https://www.wordstream.com/blog/ws/2018/02/06/real-estate-facebook-ads

Facebook Ads For Restaurants: 6 Killer Ad Strategies. (2019). 39 Celsius Web Marketing Consulting. Retrieved 13 March 2019, from https://www.39celsius.com/Facebook-ads-for-restaurants-5-killer-ad-strategies/

Adkins, T. (2018). How to Use Facebook Ads for Local Businesses. Social Media Marketing | Social Media Examiner. Retrieved 13 March 2019, from https://www.socialmediaexaminer.com/how-to-use-Facebook-ads-for-local-businesses/

The Importance of Facebook Marketing for Small Business - AMMEX. (2018). AMMEX. Retrieved 13 March 2019, from https://blog.ammex.com/the-importance-of-Facebook-marketing-for-small-business/#.XIh8WegzbIV

Get started with Business Manager: Free guide. (2019). Facebook Business. Retrieved 13 March 2019, from https://www.facebook.com/business/learn/how-business-manager-works/guide

How to Set Up a Fan Page in 5 Easy Steps. (2013). Heyo Blog. Retrieved 13 March 2019, from https://blog.heyo.com/how-to-set-up-a-fan-page-in-5-easy-steps/

22 Facebook Marketing Tips for Small Businesses on a Budget. (2019). Wordstream.com. Retrieved 13 March 2019, from https://www.wordstream.com/blog/ws/2018/07/02/faceboo k-marketing-for-small-business

Enterprise, F., Agencies, F., Business, F., Management, F., Marketing, F., & Care, F. et al. (2016). Facebook Fan Page vs. Profile: Know the Difference. Sprout Social. Retrieved 13 March 2019, from https://sproutsocial.com/insights/Facebook-fan-page/

How to Create a Facebook Business Page in 8 Simple Steps. (2018). Hootsuite Social Media Management. Retrieved 13 March 2019, from https://blog.hootsuite.com/steps-to-create-a-Facebook-business-page/

How to Create a Facebook Group (and Build an Engaged Community). (2017). Buffer Marketing Library. Retrieved 13 March 2019, from https://buffer.com/library/Facebook-group

Gurner, J. (2018). Top 25 Real Estate Facebook Posts from the Pros & Why They Work. Fit Small Business. Retrieved 13 March 2019, from https://fitsmallbusiness.com/real-estate-facebook-posts/

10 Ways to Use Facebook Groups for Restaurants - Social Chefs. (2016). Social Chefs. Retrieved 13 March 2019, from http://www.socialchefs.com/Facebook-groups-for-restaurants/

(2019). Retrieved from https://www.socialbakers.com/blog/219-top-10-biggest-mistakes-you-make-on-Facebook-pages

10 Common Facebook Marketing Mistakes (and How to Avoid Them) - dummies. (2019). dummies. Retrieved 13 March 2019, from https://www.dummies.com/business/marketing/social-media-marketing/10-common-Facebook-marketing-mistakes-and-how-to-avoid-them/

Haydon, J. (2015). 13 Super Creative Ways to Boost Facebook Page Reach - Without Facebook Ads. John Haydon. Retrieved 13 March 2019, from https://www.johnhaydon.com/13-ways-boost-your-Facebook-reach-without-spending-dime/

Bramble, J. (2018). 13 Facebook Engagement Tactics for Your Business Page. Social Media Marketing | Social Media Examiner. Retrieved 13 March 2019, from https://www.socialmediaexaminer.com/13-Facebook-engagement-tactics-business-page/

Garst, K. (2018). 17 Killer Facebook Post Ideas for Small Business Owners. Kim Garst | Marketing Strategies that WORK. Retrieved 13 March 2019, from https://kimgarst.com/17-killer-Facebook-post-ideas-for-small-business-owners/

22 Facebook Post Ideas for Businesses that Practically GUARANTEE Engagement. (2019). Postplanner.com. Retrieved 13 March 2019, from https://www.postplanner.com/Facebook-post-ideas-for-businesses-that-guarantee-engagement/

Trends, S., "Like", 2., & Pilon, A. (2017). 20 Facebook Post Ideas Your Small Business Fans Will "Like" - Small Business Trends. Small Business Trends. Retrieved 13 March 2019, from https://smallbiztrends.com/2017/04/Facebook-post-ideas.html

22 Facebook Marketing Tips for Small Businesses on a Budget. (2019). Wordstream.com. Retrieved 13 March 2019,

from
https://www.wordstream.com/blog/ws/2018/07/02/faceboo
k-marketing-for-small-business

5 Biggest Mistakes You're Making on Your Facebook Business Page. (2015). AP Digital. Retrieved 13 March 2019, from https://www.absoluteperfectionmedia.com/5-biggest-Facebook-business-page-mistakes/

Pelletreau, C. (2018). Create Scroll-Stopping FB Ads. Claire Pelletreau. Retrieved 13 March 2019, from https://clairepells.com/create-scroll-stopping-fb-ads/

works, H., Agencies, F., e-Commerce, F., Businesses, F., Advertiser, F., & Features, A. et al. (2015). 5 Ways To Get Your Posts More Attention In The News Feed. AdEspresso. Retrieved 13 March 2019, from https://adespresso.com/blog/5-ways-get-posts-attention-news-feed/

Kim, L., & Kim, L. (2015). The Science Behind Why People Engage with Facebook Content [INFOGRAPHIC]. Social Media Today. Retrieved 13 March 2019, from https://www.socialmediatoday.com/news/the-science-behind-why-people-engage-with-facebook-content-infographic/454653/

Enterprise, F., Agencies, F., Business, F., Management, F., Marketing, F., & Care, F. et al. (2018). How to Master Facebook Ad Targeting & Zero-In on Your Audience. Sprout Social. Retrieved 13 March 2019, from https://sproutsocial.com/insights/Facebook-ad-targeting/

Tariq, I. (2019). 5 Ways Your Business May Not (But Should) Be Taking Advantage of Facebook Marketing. Entrepreneur. Retrieved 13 March 2019, from https://www.entrepreneur.com/article/325277

How to Use Facebook Business Manager: A Step-by-Step Guide. (2018). Hootsuite Social Media Management. Retrieved 13 March 2019, from https://blog.hootsuite.com/Facebook-business-manager-guide/

5 Reasons You Should Be Advertising on Facebook. (2019). Wordstream.com. Retrieved 13 March 2019, from https://www.wordstream.com/blog/ws/2015/10/14/advertising-on-facebook

How to Use Facebook Business Manager: A Step-by-Step Guide. (2018). Hootsuite Social Media Management. Retrieved 13 March 2019, from https://blog.hootsuite.com/Facebook-business-manager-guide/

Hubbel, A. (2017). 5 Benefits of the Facebook Pixel | AdvertiseMint. AdvertiseMint. Retrieved 13 March 2019, from https://www.advertisemint.com/5-benefits-of-the-Facebook-pixel/

How to Advertise on Facebook: The Complete Guide. (2018). Hootsuite Social Media Management. Retrieved 13 March 2019, from https://blog.hootsuite.com/how-to-advertise-on-

Facebook/#howto

works, H., Agencies, F., e-Commerce, F., Businesses, F., Advertiser, F., & Features, A. et al. (2017). Mobile and Desktop Ads? Elevate Your Facebook Campaign and Use Both. AdEspresso. Retrieved 13 March 2019, from https://adespresso.com/blog/mobile-and-desktop-ads/

9 Tips to Write the Best Facebook Ads Ever (with Examples). (2019). Wordstream.com. Retrieved 13 March 2019, from https://www.wordstream.com/blog/ws/2016/06/29/best-facebook-ads

West, T. (2019). 4 Reasons Why You Need A Content Calendar. Blog.scrunch.com. Retrieved 13 March 2019, from https://blog.scrunch.com/4-reasons-why-you-need-a-content-calendar

7 Ways to STOP Wasting Time & Money on Facebook Marketing. (2019). Postplanner.com. Retrieved 13 March 2019, from https://www.postplanner.com/ways-to-stop-wasting-time-money-on-Facebook-marketing/

How to Create a Social Media Content Calendar: Tips and Templates. (2018). Hootsuite Social Media Management. Retrieved 13 March 2019, from https://blog.hootsuite.com/how-to-create-a-social-media-content-calendar/

Gingerich, M. (2016). Get the Maximum Facebook Ad Results with Minimal Ad Management. Neal Schaffer-Social Media Speaker, Author, Consultant, Educator and Influencer.

Retrieved 13 March 2019, from https://nealschaffer.com/how-to-get-the-maximum-Facebook-ad-results-with-minimal-ad-management/

Owens, R. (2018). How to Combine Facebook Ads and Email Marketing for Better Conversions. Social Media Marketing | Social Media Examiner. Retrieved 13 March 2019, from https://www.socialmediaexaminer.com/Facebook-ads-email-marketing/

Hiban, P. (2019). 4 Tips For Effective Real Estate Email Marketing. Inman. Retrieved 13 March 2019, from https://www.inman.com/2017/06/05/4-tips-for-effective-email-marketing/

Chef, T., Chef, T., & Chef, T. (2018). Retrieved 13 March 2019, from https://upserve.com/restaurant-insider/quick-restaurant-email-marketing-best-practices/

Here Are 5 Reasons Why Email Marketing Still Matters. (2014). Inc.com. Retrieved 13 March 2019, from https://www.inc.com/peter-roesler/top-5-reasons-why-email-marketing-is-still-works.html

Thiefels, J., & Thiefels, J. (2018). 8 Straight-Forward Content Marketing Tips for Small Businesses. Jessica Thiefels | Organic Content Marketer. Retrieved 13 March 2019, from https://jessicathiefels.com/Organic-Content-Marketer-Blog/content-marketing-small-businesses/

Developing your USP: A step-by-step guide. (2019). Marketingdonut.co.uk. Retrieved 13 March 2019, from https://www.marketingdonut.co.uk/marketing-strategy/branding/developing-your-usp-a-step-by-step-guide

Stelzner, M. (2017). Using Facebook Ads to Turn New Customers Into Repeat Customers. Social Media Marketing | Social Media Examiner. Retrieved 13 March 2019, from https://www.socialmediaexaminer.com/using-Facebook-ads-to-turn-new-customers-into-repeat-customers-maxwell-finn/

Digital organizing 101: What is a ladder of engagement and why do I need one?. (2016). Medium. Retrieved 13 March 2019, from https://medium.com/@jack_milroy/digital-organizing-101-what-is-a-ladder-of-engagement-and-why-do-i-need-one-c523b5874e16

6 Ways to Use Emotional Storytelling as a Marketing Strategy. (2016). 3 Door Digital. Retrieved 13 March 2019, from http://3doordigital.com/6-tips-using-emotional-storytelling-marketing-strategy/

9 Great Tips for Stopping Social Media Scrolling in its Tracks. (2019). Solutionreach.com. Retrieved 13 March 2019, from https://www.solutionreach.com/blog/9-great-tips-for-turning-heads-with-your-social-media-posts

Marketing, C. (2017). How To Choose Scroll-Stopping Blog Images - Content Curation Marketing. Content Curation Marketing. Retrieved 13 March 2019, from http://www.contentcurationmarketing.com/how-to-choose-scroll-stopping-blog-images/

Facebook Video Tips: 12 Ideas for More Engagement. (2018).

Search Engine Journal. Retrieved 13 March 2019, from https://www.searchenginejournal.com/Facebook-video-tips/238911/

Hutchinson, A., & Hutchinson, A. (2016). Facebook Adds New Tools to Amplify Word-of-Mouth Recommendations, Boost Response. Social Media Today. Retrieved 13 March 2019, from https://www.socialmediatoday.com/social-business/Facebook-adds-new-tools-amplify-word-mouth-recommendations-boost-response

Holmes, J. (2018). 10 Ways to Make Your Content Marketing Go Viral. Jeffbullas's Blog. Retrieved 13 March 2019, from https://www.jeffbullas.com/10-ways-make-content-marketing-go-viral/

11 Tips to Improve Your Facebook Ad Conversions. (2018). Hootsuite Social Media Management. Retrieved 13 March 2019, from https://blog.hootsuite.com/improve-Facebook-ad-conversions/

What Types of Content Are Going to Work Best in 2018?. (2018). Core dna. Retrieved 13 March 2019, from https://www.coredna.com/blogs/best-types-of-content

Johnson, W., & Johnson, W. (2019). 10 Ways to Find Inspiration for Your Social Media Posts | RankWatch Blog. Blog.rankwatch.com. Retrieved 13 March 2019, from https://blog.rankwatch.com/10-ways-to-find-inspiration-for-your-social-media-posts/#-for-your-social-media-posts/

www.ingramcontent.com/pod-product-compliance
Lightning Source LLC
LaVergne TN
LVHW022317060326
832902LV00020B/3513